THE NOVEL AND THE
OXFORD MOVEMENT

THE NOVEL AND THE OXFORD MOVEMENT

BY

JOSEPH ELLIS BAKER

NEW YORK
RUSSELL & RUSSELL · INC
1965

FIRST PUBLISHED IN 1932
REISSUED, 1965, BY RUSSELL & RUSSELL, INC.
BY ARRANGEMENT WITH PRINCETON UNIVERSITY PRESS
L.C. CATALOG CARD NO: 65—18788
PRINTED IN THE UNITED STATES OF AMERICA

TO MY MOTHER

CONTENTS

PREFACE

PARTICULARLY FOR SCEPTICS AND ANGLO-CATHOLICS

THE Victorian English left us, in the form of fiction, a picture of themselves more complete than any we possess for other nations or other generations. But historians have almost ignored this vast mine of humane knowledge, a source of insight, if not indeed of fact. The view of an intellectual movement presented by men of unquestioned honesty to a public too well acquainted with the subject to accept obvious misrepresentation, should be valuable—not only for what is stated, but also for what is unconsciously revealed of bias, assumption, of the spiritual atmosphere of the time. Moreover, the Victorians were tremendously concerned with religion, lest it vanish, and their chief instrument of propaganda (in fact, their favorite means of presenting serious psychological or social study) was the novel. It was, furthermore, their most popular art. Yet the nineteenth-century novel, like Elizabethan drama, was hardly considered serious literature by contemporary critics, and even in the succeeding decades met with patronizing tolerance among literary dogmatists. We understand Shakespeare, Jonson, and Marlowe much better after a century of humble research among the minor Elizabethans, but the same work has not yet been done for the Victorian novel. Both history and criticism might ultimately profit by some patient plowing of this ground.

My object has been to let the fiction throw light on the Oxford Movement, and conversely, to add to our knowledge of the Victorian novel by showing the different kinds of treatment it accorded to one special subject through the changing fashions of two generations. I have covered only the novels of contemporary manners which reflect the Oxford Movement, and only in so far as they reflect the Movement.[1] The most important historical novels written in that period have been added because they contribute to our knowledge of the currents of thought in the nineteenth century itself. Another word as to limits: I have seldom given synopses. The mere story is usually for our present purposes unimportant. A synopsis is often a bore, and not even an instructive bore, for it bears about as much relation to the work of art as the description of a block of marble might bear to a statue. Where I have sketched the plot, it is because this has some significance *per se*. Frequently, the only thing of interest to us in a character is one of his remarks—it would be impossible to tell about his birth and childhood, who married him and why her father did not want her to, and how this virtuous unfortunate finally inherited an estate and became a gentleman.

Sometimes I have had to work as a pioneer. Even bibliographies are lacking, and occasionally it was necessary to work out for myself methods that tradition would have supplied for the elder periods or for the better-studied literary genres. Moreover, scholarship is mere pedantry until it offers tentative conclusions, for only generalizations can be *used* in thinking. But the very subject-matter of humanistic research forces us to base our generalizations, always, on incomplete material. The result is a map drawn on the basis of what can be descried of a broken landscape. We can only lay down a rough path which may later be improved or perhaps abandoned.

[1] I have not surveyed juvenile fiction because it is of little interest for our purposes, either for its artistic form or for its picture of the Movement.

There were two other obstacles. One of them was solved with comparative ease. No American library had enough material to provide a sufficient background for this study. But that was remedied by half a year in the British Museum and the Bodleian Library, combined with the use, previously, of the New York Public Library, the Princeton Theological Seminary Library, the university libraries of Princeton, Illinois, and Columbia, and generous loans from the Boston Public Library, the Mercantile Library of Philadelphia, the Library Company of Philadelphia, the Harvard University Library, and the Enoch Pratt Free Library, Baltimore. To all of these libraries, and to the Bibliothèque Nationale and the Bibliothèque Ste-Geneviève, of which I made some use, I am very grateful.

The other obstacle sprang from the delicate nature of my subject. It touches a controversy still very lively, a matter of religion tender to the hearts of many of my friends. Doubtless each school of opinion might find in this record ammunition for its own side, and perhaps pick up a few hints on the technique of fictional propaganda. But I have attempted to preserve, on my own part, an attitude of almost inhuman detachment and to remain austerely objective. I have given all sides their say. Nevertheless, I have found the rôle of Zeus harder to play than I expected, especially since it is necessary, in dealing with this kind of material, to exercise the function of critic. In attempting to avoid prejudice, I have perhaps leaned over backwards. But let the Roman Catholics remember that statements which seem to them the fruit of heretical principles, might appear to a Puritan rank Jesuitry. I can only hope that Anglo-Catholics will all be more interested in seeing how far Progress has carried them from their recent predecessors than in searching for evidence of insufficient zeal in the narrator. I have felt that the sensibilities of the sceptics would be, of all,

the most difficult to avoid offending, and that, though I expect
to escape the Papal Index, the Evangelical pulpits and the
Boston censors, I may yet be quoted in the *Mercury's* "Ameri-
cana." For there is an Intolerance today which thinks any attention to religion, unless hostile, merely a waste of time. A plea
to this group is to be made, not in the name of faith, but of
culture. Political history is often interpreted with incredible
naïveté by those ignorant of the force of religion. Drop religion
from your Humanities, and you cease to understand Dante, or
Milton, or Raphael. You miss much in Gothic architecture, in
Goethe, in Shakespeare, and even your enjoyment of Hardy
and Voltaire is diminished. Some of our richest psychological
knowledge is recorded in theological language, for when a
great man is discussing with profound insight his own experience and conception of reality, he is sure to probe deeply into
the human mind, even as secularly conceived. Whether one likes
it or not, even the shallowest philosophy cannot ignore the fact
that the human mind is profoundly desirous of self-sacrifice,
and that to follow the supernatural life—to renounce all the
instincts that make for survival in the natural world (desire
for sexual love, ambition, individual liberty) often brings a
peace that passeth understanding. Obedience to something that
appeals neither to sense, nor desire, nor reason, an obedience
passionate beyond passion, the ecstasy of martyrdom that some
have found in fighting for revolutions, and others in torture
of the flesh—these are the hard, ineradicable data in man's
record, and might well justify a feeling of wonder at the mysteriousness of life, at the strange failure of every reasonable
system by which the mind has tried to make believable all
that its intuition knows to be real. Some fear to study religion,
I suspect, because they hold their scepticism with no firm
faith, and are afraid of being seduced. Others, fiercely pro-

saic, have a dizzy horror of bottomless chasms and lonely vastnesses. But is it not the duty of scholars to wage unremitting warfare against obscurantism of all sorts, radical as well as traditionary, Bohemian as well as pedantic?—to keep any kind of hard crust from forming around the human spirit?

I owe a great debt to the advice of Professor T. M. Parrott and Professor G. H. Gerould, of Princeton University, who read this book in manuscript. I have also made use of important suggestions offered by Professor R. K. Root and Mr. M. O. Young, of Princeton, Professor L. Cazamian of Paris, Professor E. Bernbaum, Professor R. B. Weirick, and Professor H. S. V. Jones, of the University of Illinois. These I thank again, as well as many whom I have not mentioned here.

PART I. CONTROVERSIAL FICTION

CHAPTER I

INTRODUCTION

IN THE second quarter of the nineteenth century, after an
age of free-thinking had produced a series of liberal advances ranging from the American and French Revolutions to
the English Reform Bill of 1832, there arose a counter-move-
ment which used indeed the methods of the radical propagandists but advocated a return to order, discipline, and obedience, the preservation of established institutions, and a deeper
reverence for ancient ways. In English politics this took the
form of a New Toryism, led by Disraeli. In religion it appeared as the Oxford Movement,[1] a renewal of emphasis upon
the Catholic elements that remained in the Church of England
in spite of the Reformation. In 1833 the liberal principles
which had triumphed in the Reform Bill were threatening
clerical privileges in the form of a bill to reduce the number
of bishoprics in Ireland. Though the money saved was to be
applied to other ecclesiastical purposes, John Keble preached

[1] Though usage has been loose, for clarity I have followed the practice
which confines the terms "Tractarian" and "Puseyite" to the first generation of the Oxford Movement. "Puseyite" is derived from the name of one
of the "Tractarian" leaders, and I have used the two terms as synonyms.
"Ritualism" did not become a definite movement or phase of the movement until the next generation. (See Part III.) "Anglo-Catholic" refers
to the religion as such, without regard to time. "High Church" includes
even those of the old Protestants who disliked enthusiasm. "Oxford Movement" is still the name of the whole Anglo-Catholic revival, at least until
the end of the century.

vigorously against the bill, in the Assize sermon before Oxford University on July 14. This was considered by Newman[2] the first event in the Movement.

Between a Catholic revival and opposition to a liberal reform that would have pleased Romanists in Ireland the affiliation may not at first glance seem obvious today. But it was very clear to the reactionaries of the 'thirties. The Catholic conception is that a Church must be independent of merely human governments. It would have been difficult to defend the Anglican bishoprics in Ireland on the basis of utility. In Kingsley's *Alton Locke* (1850), wonder is expressed "how Irish bishops can reconcile it to their consciences to leave behind them, one and all, large fortunes . . . saved from the fees and tithes, taken from the pockets of a Roman Catholic population, whom they have been put there to convert to Protestantism for the last three hundred years—with what success, all the world knows."[3] But the new defenders of the English Church took higher grounds than the merely utilitarian. Keble's sermon of protest was entitled "National Apostasy," and was a thorough denunciation of England, based on the doctrine that the clergy derive rights from Apostolical Succession which no man may touch without inviting the wrath of God. Nigel Penruddock (representing Manning) says in Disraeli's *Endymion,* "No human power has the right to destroy a bishopric."[4]

A. P. Perceval speaks of the proposed reform as "that wanton act of sacrilege."[5] He asks us to call to mind the actual condition of the English Church and nation at that time.

---

[2] *Apologia,* Ch. I. Supported by Church, *Oxford Movement,* I; and Perceval, *Collection of Papers,* II. These men were all leaders in the Movement.

[3] II, xiv, 3 (See below, Bibliography, II, as to method of indicating volume, chapter, and page.)

[4] I, xiv, 117.

[5] *Collection of Papers,* II, 10.

"An agrarian and civic insurrection against the bishops and clergy, and all who desired to adhere to the existing institutions of the country;—the populace, goaded on openly by speeches, covertly (as it was fully believed at the time) by the paid emissaries of the ministers of the Crown; the chief of those ministers in his place in Parliament bidding the bishops set their houses in order; the mob taking him at his word, and burning to the ground the palace of the Bishop of Bristol. . . ." This mob was declaring that it thirsted for the blood of the king. It was "headed by the descendants of the regicides of the seventeenth century, who stalked forth from their hiding-places, boasted in open day of their (base) descent, and declared their readiness to repeat the deed of their ancestors;" while the king had for his only counsellor one "who, according to uncontradicted report, had been the only member of the English House of Commons who refused to appear in mourning on the murder of Louis XVI." Even the House of Lords, "the last earthly prop of the constitution," was beginning to yield to the storm. This, according to Perceval, was the condition of England when, following Keble's sermon, a number of churchmen drew together and decided to write a series of tracts expounding the Catholic principles of the Church of England.[6] This series, called "Tracts for the Times," was what won for this first generation of the Oxford Movement the name of "Tractarian." Perhaps it would merely be necessary to educate the public, for in the House of Commons, according to one novelist, there may not have been any deliberately infidel purpose, whatever the deficiency "in information, or in rectitude of judgment, or in abiding sense of the unapproachable majesty of hallowed things."[7]

Propaganda setting forth the claims of the Church to divine

[6] *Collection of Papers,* III, 25-26.
[7] Harris, E.F.S., *Rest in the Church,* IV, 233.

sanction as the "English branch of the Holy Catholic Church,"
with a more vigorous assertion of the supernatural rights and
powers conferred upon episcopal clergymen at ordination, could
possibly save the Church from the reformers and England
from apostasy. That Parliament might be thwarted in its attempt to apply "to ecclesiastical purposes the revenue hitherto appropriated to the families of prelates"[8] in Ireland was a
matter of secondary importance. It was the principle of the
thing that counted. The nation, growing daily more liberal,
could not be allowed to dictate to the Church it was supposed
to obey. The Oxford Movement was well launched, though
it failed to defeat the Irish Church Bill.

Keble's sermon, and even the "Tracts," were probably little
more than the occasion for a crystallization of existing, though
perhaps dormant, sentiment in favor of Catholicism. For
among the spiritual roots of this revival have been named the
Medievalism of the Romantic period, especially of Scott's
novels,[9] and even the religious seriousness of the Evangelicals.[10]
The difference between the Anglo-Catholics and the greater
portion of English Churchmen was and is, briefly, the difference between the Catholic and Protestant. The Oxford Movement did not reveal its full potentialities immediately, but in
time it had insisted on the doctrine of Apostolical Succession, on the importance of the Sacraments (with Mass as the
central act of worship), on confession and absolution. It led to
the establishment of monastic institutions, to some practice of
celibacy among the clergy, and to hope for reconciliation with
Rome.

[8] Cornish, *The English Church in the Nineteenth Century,* I, 230.
[9] See quotations from Borrow below, Ch. VIII. See also Liddon, *Life
of Pusey,* I, 254; Thureau-Dangin, *La Renaissance Catholique en Angleterre,* I, p. xii, note I; Gates, *Three Studies in Literature,* 113; Cross,
Development of the English Novel, 211.
[10] Liddon, *Life of Pusey,* I, 254f; Newman, *Apologia.*

The Movement, in spite of its relations to broad streams of national life, ripened for a decade within academic walls. There it produced the "Tracts" and young clergymen fired with a new zeal, until the storm aroused by Newman carrying Catholic interpretation too far in Tract 90,[11] and, four years later, his secession to the Church of Rome, burst the pod, cleared the way at Oxford for liberals like Jowett, and left to germinate in many corners of England the seeds of "Puseyism."[12] When it went forth into the world, the Movement grew more practical, and, gradually, less doctrinal.[13] We have nothing later to correspond to the "Tracts," but instead a weekly paper, the *Guardian*, begun in the year following Newman's secession, with its office not at Oxford but in London; we have the founding of sisterhoods, protests against legal decisions that favored Protestants or Liberals, and, in many parishes of town and country, clergymen of the English Church encouraging practices that most of the bishops considered too Catholic. Important as fiction was in the 'forties for purposes of controversy, it is not surprising that meanwhile the "Tractarians" or "Puseyites" had begun to preach their doctrines by means of novels. Ultimately, the methods of revolutionaries proved fruitful, and "the pen of 'Puseyism' was found more than a match for the patronage of Evangelicalism."[14]

For several years after the Movement began at Oxford, almost everyone elsewhere still considered the English Church Protestant. In fact, it was then dominated by the Low Church party, the "Evangelicals", so Protestant that they considered Dissenters allies. Product of the same earlier revival of enthusiasm which produced Methodism, the Evangelicals were thought of by the general public as the opponents within the

[11] In 1841.
[12] Hutton, "The Oxford Movement," *Cambridge History*, XII, 289.
[13] Thureau-Dangin, *op. cit.*, II, 74-77; Church, *op. cit.* XIX, 351.
[14] Harris, E.F.S., *Rest in the Church*, III, 157.

Church not of the Tractarians but of the easy-going, fox-hunting parsons of the old eighteenth-century school,[15] "High Church" indeed but "High and Dry," very different, in their cold common sense and love of ease, from the new High Churchmen of the Oxford Movement.

From the end of the eighteenth century, religious stories had been written by Evangelicals, such as Hannah More and Mrs. Sherwood. But the Oxford Movement, until nearly a decade after its inception, seems to have been almost ignored by writers of fiction—confirmatory evidence that in the religious life of England it played as yet no important part. Disraeli, who was to be strongly influenced by the Movement, had used the word "Catholic" to mean "Roman Catholic" in *Contarini Fleming* (the year before Keble's sermon). That seems to have been the almost universally accepted meaning of the word at the time. In *The Converts* (1837, anon.) and in Agnew's *Geraldine* (completed 1839), the opposition is still between (Roman) Catholic and Protestant (including Anglican), though Agnew does recognize that the division is not now so clear-cut.[16]

In 1837 appeared an important clerical novel by the daughter of a clergyman and related in several ways to the fiction that was to come; yet it exhibited no trace of the Oxford Movement: Mrs. Trollope's *The Vicar of Wrexhill*. In this a Low Church clergyman is satirized from the point of view of the old High and Dry orthodoxy. Mr. Cartwright, a vicar, is odious for those qualities which the hostile novelists (including Dickens and Thackeray) usually ascribed to the extreme Protestants: cant, unctuousness, hypocrisy, smooth

[15] These older High and Dry clergymen and their work are portrayed in Gresley, *Charles Lever,* II, and Disraeli, *Endymion,* I, vi. Jane Austen has made them immortal.

[16] E.g. I, ix, 150.

success with women, the use of God's name in his own service. He practices nothing less than "a certain graduated love-making to every woman within his reach, not too poor, too old, or too ugly."[17] Especially he employs religious excitement to gain power over females, and thus he wins a wealthy widow. But, after marriage, his victim is undeceived and, when she dies, leaves him nothing. The authoress makes very clear her disapproval of entrusting to women the control of their own money, because the sex is too susceptible to religious fraud. The novel is written with a great deal of wit, and some of the turns of phrase are deadly.

> Mrs. Richards [who remained cold to the vicar] had been refused bread by a converted baker; beer, by an elected brewer; and soap and candles, by that pious, painstaking, prayerful servant of the Lord, Richard White, the tallow-chandler.[18]

Wicked humor! But the Evangelical vicar is treated with such an utter lack of sympathy that he is a mere caricature. With more psychological penetration the authoress presents the effects of religion (here Calvinism) upon the excitable imagination of women and girls. Fanny Mowbray's letter to Mary Richards[19] is an interesting acount of the feelings of a fanatic living in a world of imagination, with the revelation of an underlying strain of erotic excitement. Mrs. Trollope despises enthusiasm, and has little in common with the Oxford Movement except the Evangelical enemy. Like the later Tractarian writers, she attacks the doctrines of election[20] and regeneration[21] and asserts through one of her favorite characters that the Church has already framed prayers for every

[17] I, xv, 287.
[18] II, ix, 171-172. For another example, see I, xv, 307.
[19] III, viii, 154.
[20] See quotation above.
[21] I, xv, 307.

exigency.[22] But she differs from the Tractarians in matters of central importance. Besides her dislike of fervor, she uses the word "saint" with sarcasm, emphasizes the duty of following the religion of one's fathers, assumes that revelation harmonizes with reason and good sense, and implies that only villains scorn the good things of the world. Charles, the son of the victimized widow, praises the *true* Church-of-England religion, *which he calls Protestant.*[23] Interference of the clergy in the personal and family life of the parishioners is represented as a great evil.

So far as this novel is concerned, Anglo-Catholicism might not yet have been born, but it was already a lusty infant, offspring of the orthodox doctrines of the High Church and the enthusiastic spirit of the Low. Mrs. Trollope's novel is really for us a farewell to the old order, where such a union was not to be thought of! As if it actually stood at the end of the period past rather than at the beginning of the new, it is written with a power in fusing religious controversy and love story that the Anglo-Catholic novel was to grope for all through the 'forties. In style, humor, situations, narrative movement, and general literary merit it surpasses any novel dealing primarily with the clergy that we shall come upon in the next decade. But blundering as the first novels of the new group were to be, it is interesting to follow the gradual development of their method. And they betray a connection between Tractarianism and Tory economics not hitherto revealed by the historians of the Oxford Movement.

[22] I, xiv, 262.
[23] II, xi.

CHAPTER II

TALES FOR THE TIMES: EARLY ANGLO-CATHOLIC FICTION

"It is ten years since two gay maidens put up the celebrated petition, 'Aunt, *do* tell us what Puseyism is,—we can't get on at Almack's without being able to talk about it!' If the fair questioners had waited a little, it would have been unnecessary to trouble their good kinswoman; for them, and for all who might wish to acquire the current controversial small-talk without the labour of reading grave works of theology, the press was about to provide abundant instruction in the shape of novels and story-books, illustrating the doctrines and practices of the newly-risen 'ism.' And now a very extensive literature of this kind has grown up among us, exhibiting the 'movement' and the 'developement' in all their phases, and adding largely to the materials which must be mastered by the future Church historian who would qualify himself for describing the workings of the late controversies on the mind of our generation. Mr. Gresley and Mr. Paget are, we believe, the acknowledged fathers of this literature; . . ."[1]

T HE school of fiction spoken of here is not distinguished from its contemporaries so much by form as by subject matter. The propaganda or purpose novel had, by that time, a long past, and in the 'forties the novel of social reform, represented by Dickens, was reaching its height. Indeed, Miss Yonge and Miss Sewell, the successors in the 'fifties of Paget and Gresley as Anglo-Catholic novelists, did not use the same

[1] "Religious Stories," *Fraser's Magazine,* XXXVIII, ccxxiv, Aug. 1848, p. 150.

form at all but rather the domestic novel that came into vogue after *Vanity Fair*.[2] Even theological fiction was not a novelty, since Evangelicals had already been employing it for almost half a century. When a Victorian looked upon Gresley and Paget as innovators, his justification lay in the fact that these novelists were treating new subject matter. Since they were consciously doing something new, and were attempting to write fiction suitable to the religion they advocated, they were to a certain extent pioneers in form. Indeed, they began by trying to dispense with the love-interest, and they did not consider themselves novelists or romancers at all. This departure, together with an interest primarily in theology rather than literature, and indeed, a sad lack of artistic skill, produced a type of fiction which at first was little more than exposition and dialogue in the loosest narrative frame.

By glancing briefly at the very minor novels, both *pro* and *con*, that deal with the Oxford Movement during the 'forties, we can see the sort of thing that was being done, the ideas that were taken up, the attitude, method, the crudity of construction. At the same time the content and very bias of the novels, revealed in passing, will contribute occasional bits to our knowledge of the Oxford Movement itself, for it has often been recognized that we learn more of human history from the wingless grubs of art that cannot rise above what is peculiar to their age than from the resplendent creatures that dwell on Olympus contemplating humanity for its eternal qualities. I shall serve up for delectation representative morsels from this insignificant stew, but morsels somewhat more piquant than the average. In this first novel-by-novel discussion, I shall omit one of the most obvious features of these tales: the social, economic, and political corollary of the religious

---

[2] Completed 1848. The domestic novel is discussed in Part II below.

position. This material is best treated separately, and I have drawn it all together in another chapter. In turn, the mass of mediocre work will have established a background for a discussion of Disraeli and Newman and their treatment of the Oxford Movement. Generalizations on the methods of the fiction will be reserved, whenever possible, to the final chapter of this Part.

The new idea of using tales to advance the Oxford Movement is carefully defended in Paget's *St. Antholin's* (1841)[3] and in Paley's *Church Restorers* (1844).[4] This is indeed one of the many campaigns in that praiseworthy conquest by which prose fiction slowly won recognition as thoroughly respectable. It is a fact to be recorded in the history of criticism that as late as the middle of the nineteenth century, some writers of fiction could still feel that they must justify their art by representing it as a handmaid to theology. Others besides the Anglo-Catholics were offering the same defense.[5] Clement Walton, in Gresley's novel of that name, says that novels which treat the clergy flippantly can only be kept out of libraries if there are better works to order instead. These better works "should not be religious novels. It is impossible to avoid much unprofitable trifling in books, the main point of interest in which is some love-affair."[6] What follows is discussion in a frame-

[3] Advertisement, p. ix.
[4] Preface, p. ix.
[5] Long, *Sir Roland Ashton,* Dedication. Howard, M. M., *Brampton Rectory,* Preface, p. v.
[6] *Clement Walton,* I, 10. The word "novel" is here used with the narrower meaning of "love-story." Cf. Elizabeth Sewell, *Autobiography* XVI, 145: "Ivors . . . was my first attempt at a regular novel, or a story in which love is the essential interest." Up to that time, she says, she had attempted to show life important apart from marriage. (Of course, in this thesis, I myself am using the word "novel" in its broadest sense, according to the custom of the twentieth century.)

work of fiction, but the novel ends with a marriage, perhaps as a concession to the public.

Francis Edward Paget had already exhibited certain talent as a writer of fiction in *Caleb Kniveton, the Incendiary* (1833), a short but violent tale of a man who burns a rick yard in revenge and in doing so burns his own wife and child. He becomes an idiot. Paget's *St. Antholin's; or Old Church and New. A Tale for the Times* (1841) is concerned entirely with church restoration. One windy night, the steeple of the old church, because it was not kept in repair, fell in. An architect, who could design cheap churches, built a new one—which burned down immediately. Thus Evil is successful for a while, but in the end is thwarted by Poetic Justice and inexplicable accident. The plotting of this tale is primitive. Among the types of character that were to appear frequently in pictures of English church life, we have here the Reverend Lorenzo Bellamour, a popular preacher and lady's man,[7] the short-sighted churchwarden who is unwilling to spend money for church restoration, and a woman who at last gives money for an ideal church, that is, like the old one, but without pews. Pews were one of the special grievances of the early Tractarians, and are frequently discussed in their fiction. Paget's *Milford Malvoisin* (1842) is directed entirely against them, and bears the subtitle *Pews and Pewholders*. It contains a sarcastic description of their benefits.[8] Pews were objected to by the new enthusiasts because, besides being ugly, they emphasized class privileges in the House of God. In this novel, the poor could not find room in the church because of the space thus reserved for the luxury of the more wealthy.

Paget's growing concern with the poor appears in *The War-*

[7] VI.
[8] V, 113.

den of Berkingholt; or, Rich and Poor (1843). This is one of
the earliest of Puseyite tales to flirt with the methods of secular novels. In Chapter V, we are told that the most popular
writers of fiction are those who tell of scenes of profligacy, bru-
tality, and bloodshed. Bold thieves are made into heroes. But
why should we allow ourselves acquaintance with imaginary
characters whose actual representatives could only be com-
panions of reprobates? The public ought to demand that original talent lend its aid to instruct and amend society. Now this
tale must bring in places and characters we can have little
pleasure in contemplating, but the purpose is not merely to
amuse.—And so we are given a story of criminals attempting
to rob a house and being caught by a poor servant who has
fled the workhouse, pictures of low life, along with direct
sermons in favor of Catholicism, and scenes of respectable
clerical existence. Not only by offering us a crime story (in
order to instruct society) does this tale mark the crude beginnings of the true novel of the Oxford Movement; love-
interest is also courted under the pretense of being excluded.
"Now if this book were a novel," (that is, love-story), says
the author—talking to us about his method as he goes along—
"here would be the proper place for the writer" to tell about
Henry Flemyng being in love with Mary Clinton, "but this
book is *not* a novel, and the writer (being a confirmed bachelor) would not write an episode on Love-making for any con-
sideration;"[9]—but the suggestion has been inserted, at least.
In the end, Mary is to wed Henry, but the author leaves it to
the reader's imagination to construct the scene of the announc-
ing.[10] This novel attacks the Evangelical preachers. The Reverend Swainham, for example, is so popular with the women

[9] VI, 141-142.
[10] IX.

that he had been heard to boast of having received in one year forty-nine direct proposals and seven hundred fifty-three pairs of embroidered slippers.[11] There is a satirical sketch of Evangelical publicity, and a handbill or "bill of performance."[12] How any clergyman of the Church of England can allow himself to be seen on the same platform as dissenters (in charity work) is quite inconceivable.[13]

But Paget, though Anglo-Catholic, is far from being an extremist. He even attacks "the intolerable folly of disciples of the Tractarian school, who, in their vanity and love of notoriety have made it the apparent object of their lives to render themselves as unlike their neighbors as possible,—not in holiness, self-devotion, and *secret* acts of self-denial, but by making themselves conspicuous in externals; bowing, and crossing, and performing all manner of notable antics . . . . wearing, not crosses only, but *crucifixes* as conspicuously as possible;— writing notes to their tailor or green-grocer, and dating them . . . 'The morrow of the Translation of the Bones of St. Symphorosa;'—lighting and extinguishing candles at their prayers." They are probably simply yielding to the love of being singular wherewith Satan tempts them. "It is, of course, self-evident that such persons must be . . . but *geese*;—neither more nor less."[14] And the Warden (seemingly with the author's approval) speaks of undergraduates who come home from Oxford "full of crude crotchets of nonsense, which they call Catholicism, but which, for aught I can see, is as like Popery as one thing can be to another."[15]

Paget's tales follow the general growth in tolerance which

[11] XI, 261.
[12] VII, 160f.
[13] XI.
[14] *Warden of Berkingholt,* II, 38-39.
[15] VI, 137.

is quite noticeable by the end of the 'fifties. His *Curate of Cumberworth* and *Vicar of Roost* (both 1859) almost ignore the Tractarian controversy. Paget's naïve technique illustrates the crude beginnings of the Anglo-Catholic novel. His concern with social and economic problems will be discussed in a later chapter.

William Gresley, who shares the honor of having inaugurated the Tractarian novel, was actually more concerned than Paget with advancing Anglo-Catholicism by means of fiction. His *Clement Walton, or the English Citizen* (1840) was very early and very unsophisticated in technique among the Anglo-Catholic novels. For example, in Chapter I, the author writes, "Having made this chapter serve the double purpose of apologizing for the appearance of the present volume, and introducing our principal characters, we must now travel backwards" and give preliminary matter.[16] And on the next page, "Before commencing our story, it will be necessary, first of all, to state, in general terms, what sort of character" it is intended to delineate. This is: "one who, in all the social relations of life, acts on Christian principles."[17] This paragon is Anglo-Catholic. In him and his admiring author, early Victorian insularity and complacency reach their apogee. "He daily blessed the providence of God, which had chosen his country as the resting-place of the ark,"[18] that is, of the only true Church. In an opening lecture at the Mechanics' Institute, he outlines the theory of "a French philosopher of the last age" that man evolved from a lump of jelly without divine interposition,—"great laughter"—"another theory started by a Scotch metaphysician called Lord Monboddo" is that men were originally monkeys. "These things I mention, to shew what laughable gentlemen

[16] 12.
[17] II, 13-14.
[18] III, 30.

philosophers are, when they indulge in vain imaginings, and reject those aids which are afforded by historical records,— especially such as are found in the Sacred Volume."[19] Mr. Walton smugly preaches a certain amount of worldliness, in spite of, or as a corollary to, his piety. An Anglican clergyman, a gentleman, tells Walton that he had once entertained hopes of aspiring to the hand of the latter's daughter, but being without fortune or interest, he resolved to leave the parish. Mr. Walton says, "you have acted an honorable part, and I like you the better for it. We live in a state of society in which it is necessary for young people to be very cautious as to the attachments they form." It is folly to marry without fortune to maintain the position in life to which one is accustomed. But Walton respects the profession of the clergyman, and will give his daughter a maintenance. However, the clergyman says an Uncle in India has just died and left him an heir.[20] (Thus both men have had a chance to display the nobility of their sentiments, without losing anything by it.) In spite of this story material, the book consists chiefly of discussion.

Gresley's *Church-Clavering, or The Schoolmaster* (1843) mentions Mr. Primer, a clergyman, who might have passed for a good Churchman in his generation, but had by no means escaped the latitudinarian tendency of the age. "He had no strong feeling of the oneness and catholicity of the Church, and the great sin of those who separated themselves from it. . . . Besides, it must be remembered that we are speaking of what occurred some years since, before the real character of dissent was known;—before that violent political animosity with which they have assailed the Church, was developed. . . ."[21] (This

[19] VI, 54-55.
[20] XX, 229-231.
[21] I, 4.

betrays one reason for the Tractarians' renewing insistence upon Apostolical Succession.) Mr. Primer's son "was subjected to a trial which might have ruined a youth of less prudence and principle."[22] That is, he was tempted to enter the dissenting ministry. But Joseph, the youth of prudence and principle, went to the vicar, Mr. Andrews, who told him that "to undertake the office of minister, without the laying on of hands of the Bishop, is a presumptuous and sinful act."[23] The author, after pointing out that few people are aware of the sinfulness of schism, expresses the hope that God will make allowances when their error proceeds from ignorance. "Still schism must needs entail grievous disadvantages on those who fall into it, even without fault of their own; just as men bred and born in Roman Catholic or heathen countries labour under manifest disadvantage, from which English Churchmen have to bless God that they are exempt."[24] So Joseph becomes a schoolmaster, and the rest of the book explains directly or in dialogue the principles upon which he did his work. Gresley's *Bernard Leslie* (1842; part II, 1859) is of similar type, dialogue discussion of theological matters.

Gresley and Paget were the leading, but not the sole, Anglo-Catholic novelists of this period. Robert Armitage wrote *Doctor Hookwell; or the Anglo-Catholic Family* (1842), one of those strange fish of the early 'forties. It fills three tremendous tomes, with appendices, extensive quotations from seventeenth century divines, and reference to innumerable writers. The young ladies of a certain family are fond of getting Dr. Hookwell to deliver them lectures on some subject of Anglo-Catholic belief.

[22] I, 2.
[23] I, 7.
[24] I, 10.

A splendid morning shone on the happy party at Swanbourne
Hall, who were soon engaged in renewing their theological conversation, being desirous to "make the most" of their good and learned
friend Dr. Hookwell, while he was there.[25]

Besides the lecture, another device is the long letter written
by Dr. Hookwell, which the family eagerly opens. Our oracle
does not hastily follow the Tractarians, but supports most of
their contentions. The story contains political activity, and,
if not a love story, at least a very thin thread leading to marriage. The author's *Ernest Singleton* (1848) is similar in
structure and subject.

F. A. Paley, Honorary Secretary to the Cambridge Camden
Society, wrote a novel devoted entirely to the question of
church restoration, namely, *The Church Restorers: A Tale
treating of Ancient and Modern Architecture and Church Decoration* (1844).[26] The hero of this tale is an old church, whose
history is told from Saxon origins to nineteenth-century degradation. The preface admits that a contrast is drawn between
the Medieval and the Reformed Church, unfavorable to the
latter in respect to faith, devotion, and discipline, as well as
church architecture.[27] When the church is finally restored in
spite of "No Popery" sentiment, the parishioners are delighted
beyond measure.[28] In novels by the Evangelical opposition, on
the other hand, restoration is usually represented as emptying
the church.

Lady Georgiana Fullerton, who went over to Rome in 1846,

[25] II, viii, 260.
[26] This tale is mentioned here because of chronology, and because it illustrates the odd forms taken by early Tractarian fiction. Its esthetic
theories will be discussed in Chapter XIII below.
[27] P. vii.
[28] XIV.

at the time of writing *Ellen Middleton* (1844) still belonged
to the Tractarian party; but according to a preface of 1860
she already had gleams of Catholic truth. This is a sensational,
false, inflated novel. We have mentioned, in discussing the
pioneering of Paget, that misalliance between crime-story and
religious discussion which he produced in *The Warden of Berkingholt.* In *Ellen Middleton,* we have an attempt equally crude
but entirely different in nature—a melodramatic story is told
illustrating the need of confession. Ellen causes the death of
her cousin by an angry blow. Henry Lovell—Satanic—cultivated, charming, but withal heartless—gains control over Ellen.
Everything turns upon Ellen's keeping her crime secret, and she
is so miserable that it is incredible she should not have confessed sooner. Besides Ellen and that villain, Henry Lovell,
there are other worthy characters. There is Alice, an angel
of goodness. Her grandmother writes that she "has lived alone
with her flowers and her Bible. She has never opened a novel;
she has never conversed with any one but me, and with him
who is now her husband."[29] Ellen gives the manuscript of her
life story to one Mr. Lacy. The business of this man's life
was prayer and the exercise of charity. His few hours of
relaxation were spent in the study of ecclesiastical architecture and saints' lives. Contemptible as the novel is, it is one
of the earliest Tractarian novels to attempt not merely a fictional framework for expository discussions, but an actual
story, the very plot of which turns on a Catholic principle.

Melodrama is more successful in *Hawkstone* (1845) by
William Sewell, one of the few obscure Tractarian novels of
this period that still might afford amusement to the average
reader. Like so many of its contemporaries, this tale is a curi-

[29] VIII, 115.

ous kettle of unrelated fish: Chartists, a secret passage, con-
spiracies, a Curse, a lost son, Jesuits, Dickens-like satire, and
political arguments. The Roman Catholics are represented as
for the most part murderous villains. The hero, Villiers, will
not admit that the Romish Church is Catholic.[30] He declines
to run for Parliament because the *Conservatives* have drawn
up a program for him that is too liberal—(in tolerating dissenters and upholding the supremacy of the House of Commons).[31]
As to the heroine, readers are told they will rejoice to learn
that she is to be "a real lady, such as a heroine should be. Not
as if the middle walks of life were contemptible, and had no
joys or sorrows, duties or virtues, to excite our sympathies
and interests; but because, where goodness does exist accompanied with rank and birth, it exists in a higher and nobler
form than in an humbler station."[32] The novel also shows us
nineteenth-century life through stained-glass windows. Hostile
to industrialism, it tries to picture a society modern yet
dominated by Church and Nobility. Villiers makes over to
trustees, under control of the bishop of the diocese, the part
of the Hawkstone estate which was sacrilegiously obtained by
his ancestors from the plunder of a priory. A college of clergy
and others is established in the restored priory for the perpetual celebration of divine worship, the spiritual guardianship
of the parish, the education of the young, and the care of the
poor, sick, destitute, and penitent. Villiers also surrenders the
tithes of Hawkstone.[33] He himself becomes a paternalistic ruler,
binding down all whom he can to obtain from their own neighborhood the commodities they require. "But what Villiers was

[30] II, xiii, 173.
[31] II, xiv.
[32] I, ii, 29.
[33] II, xii, 168.

most anxious to encourage was a system of domestic manufactures, the spinning, knitting,—everything which could be carried on round the family fireside."[34]

The writing of Tractarian fiction was not even confined to adults, for *Enthusiasm Not Religion*[35] was the work of a girl not yet eighteen.[36] The purpose of this book was to show the sin of dissension in matters of religion. It attacked Low Church and Dissent with a child's bigotry. The volume is of little value, except that it illustrates the astonishing range and variety of the attempts at fiction by even obscure Tractarians.

Of higher quality, worthy to rank with Paget's *Warden of Berkingholt* or Gresley's *Clement Walton,* was *William Blake* (1848) by William Edward Heygate. It is structurally very primitive, being merely one incident after another—told with real feeling for farm life—and with sermons tacked on. Like Paget and Gresley, Heygate includes a love story but avoids elaborating it—and he is deeply concerned with a social question, this time the duty of the farmers. The Bishop points out to Mr. Blake, the farmer, the degradation of country laborers when they are not encouraged to go to church or gain instruction.[37] A farmer's other duties to his employees are indicated.

Blake's sons had never thought of religion as anything which "would make a person deviate from the usual ways of men."[38] Their former Rector, Mr. Eccles, was a good shot, good farmer, and good dining companion, a kind neighbor and ready giver to the poor, but not a teacher of Church doctrine. His successor, Mr. Lee, is High, but too wise to begin at once a

[34] II, xx, 294-295.
[35] By M.A.C. (1848).
[36] Advertisement, p. xiii.
[37] II.
[38] I, 6.

thorough change, for the people, not knowing their own Church, when they saw him obey her forgotten laws, thought that it must be Popery.[39] The rectory in Mr. Eccles' time was handsomely furnished and had "sporting pictures, and guns, and antlers." But under the new incumbent, "There was nothing good in the house except some sacred engravings," oak chairs, bookshelves, and library. There was nothing that would have made the poor afraid to sit down, but coarse table-cloth and homely fare.[40] This book touches the chief concerns of the Tractarian fiction of the first decade: church restoration, the revival of Catholic practices in the services, and care for the poor.

[39] IV.
[40] VI, 60.

CHAPTER III

THE EVANGELICAL ONSLAUGHT

THOUGH Evangelical fiction held the field before the Anglo-Catholic novel was thought of, it seems to have been some time before the Evangelicals actually turned the novel upon their new opponents. Tayler, in *Margaret* (1844),[1] makes the heroine say that she drew Tractarian doctrines "from such works as Bernard Leslie and Milford Malvoisin," and that such books ought to be called "cobwebs to catch flies." "They are a little entertaining and a little prosy, and a little sentimental, and a little witty, and very abusive." She wishes someone would answer them.[2] A glance at the Evangelical novels which attacked the Oxford Movement will make clearer the position of the Movement itself, partly because they take us into a world different culturally from that of the Anglo-Catholics, a world where style and beauty and literature are less valued, and worldly pleasures looked upon with more suspicion.

Anne Howard's *Mary Spencer: A Tale for the Times* (1844) laments that the name of Evangelical, for some years considered honorable, is beginning to be used as a term of reproach, while the name of Churchman or Catholic is coveted.[3] This novel, an attempt to remedy the situation, has for a heroine a certain kind of extreme Protestant. For example, backed

[1] Discussed below, p. 26.
[2] Part II, 110.
[3] X, 160.

by the authoress, she refuses to teach Greek mythology, saying that it seems Satan, enraged at the victory of Christ, determined to mar His triumph "and therefore devised the scheme of making pagan learning necessary in Christian schools."[4] And she says that the demon who was worshipped by the Israelites under the name of Ashtoreth "might change his name to Diana when he claimed Greek homage, and personate the Virgin Mary, when he summoned apostate christendom to his shrine."[5] She asks, "What do we want with Pascal, or Thomas à Kempis, who have the works of our own Reformers,"[6] and when a copy of The Christian Year is given to her she finds theological errors in it.[7] Another character defends an age of utility as superior to the age of romance and superstition to which many cathedrals owe their erection. It is holier to devote wealth to railroads, which will spread Christianity, than to the useless adorning of cathedrals.[8] It is implied that Puseyism is part of a Jesuit plot to win England over to Rome. When Edward Spencer found the High Church rector, Mr. Norman, interesting, another man "reproved Edward's close intimacy with a Tractarian."[9]

The same author's Ridley Seldon, or The Way to Keep Lent. A Tale for the Times (1845) contains some naïve examples of the technique of the 'forties in religious fiction. It opens with Philip Seldon sitting apart because it is Ash Wednesday, while his brother Ridley and Ridley's wife are eating a customary breakfast. Contemptuous glances failing to attract attention, Philip begins, "You are so miserably low church, Ridley, that

[4] V.
[5] V, 79-80.
[6] VII, 118.
[7] VIII, 130.
[8] IX, 134-135.
[9] XIV, 221.

I do not wonder the dissenters think they have a sort of half claim upon you." Ridley asks him for a definition of "low church."[10] The novel has very little plot, but consists of a love story interwoven with arguments and footnotes. Philip tries to introduce Tractarian story books among the children of his brother. "And so . . . is the poison of 'The Tracts for the Times,' sugared and prepared for little children."[11] Philip goes over to Rome, but is later to see his error.

Lady Catherine Long's *Sir Roland Ashton: A Tale of the Times* (1844) is ridiculously mawkish, but it shows in passing how the Tractarians looked in the eyes of those who thought them the agents of Satan. Keble's *Christian Year* had been Sir Roland's delight before Puseyism, "that fearful evil," had shown itself openly. Greek and Latin writings never satisfied Sir Roland. They do not touch the heart—and parts should never have been written. Few English poems of merit have any real religion. The portions in Milton relating to the Redeemer are too much products of imagination—he lacks realities. Now in Keble's poems there breathes a spirituality of mind, but to think that such a mind should be involved in the midst of error![12] The Tractarian doctrine is attacked by Sir Roland because it "enforces no holy separation from the world." "Fasting one day—the next at all the abominations of the theatre. What a sickening mixture!" (But a Mr. Scott tells Sir Roland to thank God for happy ignorance of the theatre.)[13] Puseyism, says Roland Ashton, is leading men from inward spiritual grace to outward forms and ceremonies. In fact, Puseyism is an additional proof that the end of this dispensa-

[10] I, 1, 2.
[11] IV (Ridley speaking).
[12] IV, 26, 27.
[13] IV, 28.

tion is at hand—the power permitted to Satan is one of the signs of the Lord's second coming. Mr. Scott says that good is also a sign of the Lord's coming, and religion flourishes now to an unprecedented degree.[14] Mr. Singleton, a paragon, does not believe the Puseyites hypocrites, but that they are blindly carrying on a work of vast incalculable evil in the world.[15] (This recognition of sincerity is important, for such admissions to the credit of an opponent are of great value in building up an historical picture.) Sir Roland approves of the Puseyites' restoration of churches, their greater degree of discipline, more frequent services in towns, improvement in music, and their attention to education.[16]

Tayler's *Margaret, or the Pearl* (1844), chiefly the story of a very pious girl, was written to warn against "one of the chief errors of the day—the heresy of Tractarianism." "I wish to show the effects of the system as it regards our own private and domestic circles."[17] (Such presentations of an abstract system in terms of human life make the novel one of the most stirring means of propaganda—in better hands.) The danger first showed its head when Margaret sang some Gregorian chants and worked upon an altar-cloth that had the head of the Virgin and the Papal banner. Other marks of Puseyism, in the new rector, were putting a lectern in the place of a reading desk, dispensing with district visitors, and forbidding the laity to read the Scriptures.[18] The congregation grew thinner. The first stone of a dissenting chapel was laid because of the rector's Tractarianism. After this, Margaret moved to a new place

[14] IV, 28, 29.
[15] X, 90.
[16] XI.
[17] Preface to first ed.
[18] Part I, 5-39.

where Mr. Steward was pastor. Under his preaching, conversion began to make itself manifest. (As opposed to baptism into the Church at birth, later conversion was the corner-stone of the Evangelical system.)

Wilkinson's *The Parish Rescued*[19] (that is, from the Tractarians) is a novel not against church decoration but against the use of symbolism, stone sedilia, marble altars, screens, rood-lofts, etc. The Puseyite schemes of Austin Oldthorpe and Mr. Pennycross, the clergyman, presented a pretty "specimen of Pagano-popish symbolism."[20] Attendance at church was reduced by what Pennycross calls obedience to the Rubrics. Theological controversy in the parish kindled strife in families. Some affected to believe that the vicar and curate were Jesuits in disguise. Mr. Lurcher, the Anglo-Catholic curate, took a deep interest in the poor and tried to introduce Catholic usages among them. Mr. Oldthorpe and the parson had a Maypole set up on the green, and encouraged skittles and football and dances for the lads and lasses after church. In honor of St. Thomas à Becket, wakes were to be held, services, music, dancing, games. But mothers came and with loud expostulations and tears implored their children to quit the unhallowed festivities. "Mr. Beaver, in a transport of zeal, rushed into the nearest cottage, borrowed an axe, and with his Bible in one hand, and the weapon in the other, made this way to the Maypole, and with half a dozen sturdy strokes levelled the abomination with the ground."[21]

In Jenner's *Steepleton* (1847), the clergyman, Frank Faithful, comes for the first time into contact with High Church

[19] Wilkinson, William Francis, *The Parish Rescued; or laymen's duties, rights, and dangers.* (1845).
[20] II, 27.
[21] III, 55-61.

clergy. He finds about them a greater air of respectability and gentlemanliness than he has been accustomed to.[22] But a dinner party shows them frivolous.[23] Faithful goes over to the Continent to see what Popery really is. This trip helps open his eyes to the real tendencies of certain principles making progress in England. The novel objects to church restoration and church tradition. It goes farthest of all in debating minute and technical problems—even the meanings of single words.

Primitive technique was not a monopoly of the Tractarians. *Trevor: or, the New St. Francis, a Tale for the Times* (1847) opens with an "audible reverie" by Henry Trevor on the elusiveness of Truth. Then,

> he arose and again muttered to himself: "To think that I, lonely from infancy, unacquainted with the simple affections which knit together the hearts of children, unpopular and unfriended at school from the reserve induced by my previous education . . . And now bewildered in doubt."[24]

But, in presenting the picture of an austere ascetic, the author shows considerable power. Malinsey, ostensibly a High Anglican curate, acts on the theory of self-annihilation, and hopes to subjugate in himself the passion of love. Crushing his instincts, he consequently develops dark jealousies. He uses his priestly influence within the Arden family until it goes farther than he wished: Mrs. Arden hints at retiring from the world. He now tries to "wean" Mrs. Arden from the ideas he has instilled. She is unconvinced. He has taught her to rely on his advice as confessor and cannot get her to free him now. The shocking comedy of this situation is handled with delicate humor, as if the author were not smiling at all. Then it is revealed that

[22] IX.
[23] XI.
[24] I, 3.

Malinsey has been for some time a member of the Roman Church masquerading in an English curacy as an Anglican. Since he has abdicated his own power to discriminate between right and wrong, his conscience has died the death. But Malinsey is not portrayed unsympathetically, and we can begin to look forward to the later novels where interesting stories grow out of the concern with some Catholic ideal. Mrs. Arden is also a good psychopathic study—a woman who has never had a real lover, married coldly, now stirred to the depths by the priest, her emotion taking the form of religion. This is one of the earliest novels I have found where Tractarianism is studied for its psychological possibilities. It is also written from a point of view more Low-Church-Liberal than violently Calvinistic.

In *Alfred Lennox* (1851), the hero of that name, indoctrinated with High Church principles by Oxford and by a tutor moving towards Rome, preaches a sermon which his sister hears. She is shocked at the Catholic emphasis on good works —as if for an act of sinful man his sins would be forgiven. "I warn you, Alfred, . . . as you believe that you must yet render an account to God, never again to tempt a weak child like me with error. . . ."[25] The novel is full of arguments, often setting forth *both* sides of the question.

Allerton and Dreux: or the War of Opinion (1851) by Jean Ingelow, takes us into a community dominated by the clergy, priest-ridden, says Rector Raeburn. Allerton is a High Church rector; Dreux, Low, has more influence, though only a curate. The novel is fair enough to portray both as fine men. But the *very* High curate, and later vicar, Hewly, is utterly despicable. It is emphasized that Hewly was not born a gentleman. Ultimately, Allerton is converted to Evangelicalism. There is

[25] P. 38.

really little war of opinion here, though that difference furnishes an obstacle to love. That the theology should play second
fiddle to the romance is one evidence that we are in the
'fifties.

Charlotte Anley in *Earlswood; or, Lights and Shadows of
the Anglican Church* (1852) allows a fair chance to each side
to present its position, though it is true that she is unable to
make any of her characters speak with much intelligence. Her
comparatively impartial method is all the more noticeable because the author herself bursts into a stupid direct tirade against
Tractarianism at the end of one of the chapters.[26] It seems to
have become by that time the fashion to represent both sides
of the question under discussion, and this practice probably exerted some pressure on the writer. This novel objects to *ladies*
going out to seek the sick down dark lanes, because it is improper.[27] That shocking practice was found among Anglo-
Catholics.

Amy Wilton (1852) by Worboise, belongs, in its crudity,
with this earlier group of novels, while her *Overdale* (1869)
belongs with those I shall discuss in Part III—a proof that a
general development can be defined, and all the more valuable
since few of our authors besides Disraeli and Yonge spread
their novels over a long period of time. In this tale, a clergyman becomes a Tractarian, but repents when near death. It is
especially emphasized that Tractarianism flatters THE PRIDE
of human nature by its doctrine of good works.[28]

*Experience; or, the Young Church-Woman. A Tale of the
Times* (1854)[29] belongs in time to the middle 'fifties, but it is
of the same school we have been tracing. It is chiefly direct

[26] VIII, 199-200.
[27] XV, 404.
[28] XII.
[29] By M.E.S.B.

narrative. It is the story of a girl's "experience" with religions, one after another, which are not Low-Church-of-Englandism. Obviously, the author has never experienced any other religion herself, for it never occurs to her that the latter might not be the only Truth. The author is bad-tempered, as well as narrow. For example, she says that one church seemed to Agnes like "some Popish mass house."[30] Agnes refuses to go to the opera, it being her rule "never to go anywhere to which I would not take my Saviour . . . *should* we like to die in such a place?"[31] Ultimately she marries a lord, and virtue is rewarded.

The Evangelical novels indicate a general belief in the sincerity and industry of the Puseyites—and considerable suspicion that they were unconsciously the tools of the fearful Jesuits, or, at least, of Satan. Opponents seem to agree with advocates in showing the Anglo-Catholics as practicing austere individual asceticism, combined with a greater toleration of worldly pleasures for those who felt no call to the holier life. Sir Roland Ashton says that nothing convinces him of the evils of those doctrines more than the change they effect on many who had formerly acted on Evangelical principles. Such people return to vain and frivolous dissipations of the world.[32] Anglo-Catholics also seem to have encouraged popular sports and amusements, even on Sunday.[33] Indeed, what the Evangelical novels have told us about the interests and activities of the Tractarians does not differ much, except in the interpretation put upon them, from what the Tractarian novelists themselves revealed. In so far as the friendly and hostile propagandists agree on tangible date, we may surely assume con-

[30] XX.
[31] XIX.
[32] *Sir Roland Ashton,* XI, 101.
[33] *Steepleton,* XX; *The Parish Rescued,* III; See also Eliza Lynn Linton's *Under Which Lord?* II, viii, 190; and her *Lizzie Lorton,* II, x.

siderable validity for the impression of the movement which remains with us after we have forgotten the flaws of the art or the spirit of the artist. At least, we have had a picture of the Oxford Movement as an event actually taking place in Victorian England, spreading far and wide into many parishes and bringing with it community strife, domestic tragedies, and a leaven of excitement over some very important theories about the conduct of human life. For all schools represent the battles between the Tractarians and their parishioners as spiteful, indeed, but based upon fundamental opposition intellectually and ethically. Let us now turn to some of the important social theories involved in the early Oxford Movement.

CHAPTER IV

ANGLO-CATHOLICISM *VERSUS* DEMOCRACY

'Tis sad to watch Time's desolating hand
  Doom noblest things to premature decay:
  The Feudal court, the Patriarchal sway
Of Kings, the cheerful homage of a land
Unskilled in treason, every social band
  That taught to rule with sweetness, and obey
  With dignity, swept one by one away
While proud Empirics rule in fell command.
Yet, Christian! faint not at the sickening sight; . . .[1]

THE Oxford Movement was not merely a reaction against Rationalism and Protestantism. Its social, political, and economic alliances (or perhaps we should call them entanglements) were even more interesting. Though in the 'fifties and 'sixties the emphasis was to be placed on the effect of Catholic principles upon the individual mind, in the 'forties the Anglo-Catholic novel was largely concerned with the Church as a solution for social evils. The Tractarian novel came to the defense of secular Toryism. The connection is almost taken for granted. In Gresley's *Bernard Leslie* (part one), the narrator says that his father, though a layman, was a very sincere member of the established Church, and had a just abhorrence of the French Revolution. He "threw all his influence to the side of order and Christianity."[2] But we do not have here the old dry

---

[1] Froude, R. H. "Farewell to Feudalism," poem CLVII of *Lyra Apostolica,* a volume of poems written by leaders of the Oxford Movement.
[2] Ch. I.

spirit of an upper class arrogantly enjoying the fruits of the earth guaranteed them by law, like Thackeray's old aristocratic dragons. Instead, we are urged to paternal care for the poor, counter-agitation, enthusiasm, an attempt to solve social problems *not* by a reorganization of society but within the existing frame (to whose support the new school brings the assertion of Divine sanction). The work of the first Oxford Movement novelists, Gresley and Paget, had the condition of England as a primary concern, and offered Catholicism not merely as a religious end in itself, but as a solution for discontent. Paget's *Warden of Berkingholt* was written, according to the preface, in the hope of prevailing on some of the upper and middle classes to think more seriously about their duties to the lower, and about the need of urgent sacrifices and self-denials if the spiritual needs of the manufacturing districts are to be cared for. "If the country is to be saved at all . . . It will, under God, be saved by the Church's influence." Evils can be remedied and the craving of our hearts eased only by the system of the Holy Catholic Church. Protestantism has been found inadequate, and it is the deceiver of souls who now tempts men with "Socialism, or Mormonism, or some kindred heresy."[3] The conclusion repeats that there is growing distress which cannot be mended by acts of Parliament or by political economy, but only by the Church. Between preface and conclusion, the tale itself does not illustrate this moral. Though the author gives us pictures of poverty and crime, and shows us the "Hospital of St. Swithuns," we see little of the inmates in the almshouse! We are instructed that the best way to provide for the poor is by giving alms into the hands of the Church, and the method used to prove this is to exhibit a selfish and wicked character who doesn't believe it. Paget's *The Pageant; or Pleas-*

[3] Pp. xiv-xvi.

ure and its Price (1843) was also written to draw the attention of the upper classes to the suffering of the poor.

In opposition to the democratic movement, the Tractarian novelists present the Tory ideal of how the lower classes should act. In Gresley's *Clement Walton,* Old Ambrose tells the story of his life: how he poached only once, and his father showed him that he was breaking some of the Ten Commandments. (The attitude towards poaching is a crucial point in these novels. The Anglo-Catholics emphasize the wickedness of the poacher and the rights of property while the liberals attack the selfishness of the wealthy preserver of game.[4]) Ambrose tells how some who went to hear a Dissenting ranter preach (which he would not do) became unsettled and took to bad and irregular ways. "Mr. Hammond was both pleased and affected by the godly simplicity of the aged Christian, and shook him cordially by the hand, promising to call and see him frequently."[5] Most flattering condescension, considering that Old Ambrose was poor! Mr. Walton says (for the author) that where the English Church has free play and development, it produces men loyal, faithful, peaceable, and intelligent. "Amongst the Dissenters . . . and . . . Presbyterians . . . there is an absence of that humble submission to authority, which is so amiable a feature of the Christian character, as developed often in the English Church; . . . Corresponding with this spiritual defect there is a political disaffection to civil government; a democratic, arrogant temper; an anxiety to maintain rights rather than to perform duties."[6] Mr. Walton points out to his groom, William, "that it is a sin against God, your heavenly Master, if you do not do your duty in whatsoever station he

[4] Cf. also *Trevor*; Kingsley's *Yeast.*
[5] Ch. IX, X, 106.
[6] X, 114-116.

has placed you," that is, keep the harness looking better.[7] Economics is elevated into the higher realm. Mr. Walton thought it a bad example to give more than the usual rate of wages. But his servants were satisfied. He had morning and evening prayers. That is part of the secret. They all felt themselves members of a common Church.[8] Mr. Walton lived in New York three years and found the principal inhabitants heartily sick of their republican government, and Mr. Hammond thinks monarchy more in accord with the Scriptures. Democracy, he thinks, develops an independent unchristian spirit, but monarchy promotes submission to law and obedience to command.[9] The author tells us that " It is as much an ordinance and decree of Divine Providence that the millions should be ruled by the few, as that a herd of oxen should submit to be driven by a child."[10] "Men have been tongue-tied by a cowardly submission to the arrogant claims of liberalism, instead of denouncing it as a cheat and imposture." But we have one safeguard—the influence of the Church. "I say, the influence of *the Church,* and not the influence of *religion* (so called); because it is manifest that whatsoever power Dissent possesses is ranged mainly on the opposite side." Already in the Church a spirit is revived, and we shall soon have enough zealous champions to "sustain the conflict against the overbearing insolence of the vaunting Goliaths of democracy." To do this, " We must provide religious instruction for the masses of our people . . . we must revive the faith, and humility, and obedience of former days. . . . If the mass of our people were sound Christian Churchmen, there would be no fear of revolution."[11]

[7] XII.
[8] XII.
[9] XIV, 160.
[10] XVI, 176.
[11] XVI, 182-185.

In Churchover, where Walton lived, "The rich were looked up to; the middle class knew their station; the poor were well cared for and contented."[12] This strikes the four notes of the new Tory economic ethics: respect for the wealthy because they have money, paternal care for the poor,—in return for which the poor are to keep quiet,—and rigid resistance to the rise of the middle class. In a meeting to discuss the corn laws, repeal is advocated by the liberal Mr. Raffles (who is later converted) and by "Mr. Junius Brutus Wiggins, formerly hair-dresser." (The note of snobbery is characteristic.) But Mr. Walton opposes repeal.[13]

Gresley's *Charles Lever; or, the Man of the Nineteenth Century* (1841) is designed to set forth the dangers to which our ill-cemented social system exposes the most numerous and important class in society.[14] Joseph Franklin, presented as an ideal yeoman, what some would call a bigot, as a consequence of reading certain passages in the Bible terminates his intimacy with his friend Lever, who is not a sound churchman. So Lever gets a new set of associates, and his son Charles has a wrong start in life. "Instead of imbibing the old English feeling of deference for his superiors, Charles was taught to abuse and ridicule the natural aristocracy of the place."[15] The Municipal Reform Act is here attacked. Trained under "A dissenting father, a latitudinarian schoolmaster, a radical magistracy, and a revolutionary and atheistical press!"[16] he grew up a democrat in politics and it is difficult to say what in religion. Farmer Franklin's son George became "a manly true-hearted Englishman,—Charles Lever, *a man of the nineteenth century.*"[17]

[12] XVII, 191.
[13] XVIII.
[14] Preface, p. v.
[15] VI, 48.
[16] VII, 54.
[17] VII, 56.

Charles even delivers a speech advocating the decimal system of coinage! He becomes a radical orator, and finds it necessary to make bold assertions without great regard for truth, and to abuse his opponents, to attract the ears of his coarse listeners. (The author, in discussing the ballot, simply assumes that to favor it is wicked or silly.) Through the influence of a politician, a Socialist gets permission from the mayor to speak in the town-hall. "Thus unconsciously was a thoughtless liberal doing the work of Satan, and prostituting his talent and station to the vilest uses . . . contributing to ruin the souls of hundreds. . . ."[18] Farmer Franklin (with the author's hearty approval) tells the Socialist that "a man might just as well take a snake into his bosom, as make acquaintance with a Socialist."[19] Lever becomes a Socialist, unable to see that social evils must be corrected by the Gospel. He deserts Christian worship, and free from all restraints of religion, falls into evil courses. A Chartist conspiracy is formed, and our hero finds himself mixed up with the schemes of the traitors. A scab-laborer is killed. Suspicion fastens on Charles. But it is found that the Union hired an outsider to do the killing. The Chartists are gathering. What could have made such as these out of those whose forefathers were England's loyal peasantry? "What but LIBERALISM? Liberalism, which, if God check it not, will ere long efface all traces of virtue and civilization from our land."[20] Lever is shot. Then the soldiers appear. Hereafter, Charles' father is a conservative. Discontent among the poorest can best be alleviated by alms given through the Church, and by saving on the part of people well-trained by the Church. Discontent among the prosperous workmen springs

[18] XI, 105.
[19] XIII, 118.
[20] XIX.

from lack of proper religious instruction. Charles does not die from his wound. Under the influence of Socialism, he once induced a young person to live with him as his wife. When he announces that he intends honourable marriage with her now, the shock causes the death of a girl of the pious Franklin family, who had watched over him in his illness. The other girl has left the country with the Socialist lecturer. Charles still continues a sincere penitent, and has resolved to lead a celibate life.

In *Bernard Leslie* (1842), the author's spokesman says that the "tangible effects" of the Tractarian doctrines "are manifold. The first great check which the democratic principle received came from them."[21] And he tells of "certain proceedings which had taken place at Oxford, partaking of a political and religious character, which had been the first serious check to the current of liberalism. . . . They proved . . . that the Tract-writers were benefactors even in a political view."[22]

Of course, Paget and Gresley were not the only Tractarian novelists who attacked democracy and other forms of radicalism. In *Doctor Hookwell* (1842) by Armitage, it is pointed out that religious liberty leads to political liberty, and therefore must be opposed. "If the standard of the Anglo-catholic theologians could be embraced by the multitude (a consummation devoutly to be wished), we should see chartism and socialism vanish away like lurid and foetid mists. . . ."[23] A certain weaver "was a hardened fellow who had embraced the new Socialistic principles," attended Dissenting chapels, and liked best the scoundrel, Mr. Gill, "for he did not fear to speak his mind about the rich."[24] In Charlotte Yonge's *Abbeychurch* (1844), the father disapproved of Mechanics' Institutes, and when a few

[21] XXI, 287.
[22] XII, 154.
[23] I, ix, quotation p. 236.
[24] II, iii, 86, 87.

Socialist lectures had been given at one, he had them stopped.[25] In *Endymion* (1880), by Disraeli, who parallels the Oxford Movement, a "great personage" says, "Now we know what Liberalism means on the continent. It means the abolition of property and religion. Those ideas would not suit this country; ...."[26] In Newman's *Callista,* a mob primarily against the Christians contains also many stimulated by "the prospect of plunder." Now "they had reached the aristocratic quarter of the city, and they gazed with envy and cupidity at the noble mansions which occupied it. They began to shout out, 'Bread, bread!' "[27] In these famished men, "the respectable quarter" of the city found an enemy almost worse than the locust. Among the liberal propositions listed by Newman, which he, "together with the High Church," "denounced and abjured" at Oxford are these: "It is lawful to rise in arms against legitimate princes" as the Puritans did in the seventeenth and the French in the eighteenth centuries. Another: "The people are the legitimate source of power."[28]

Novelists who were not Anglo-Catholic bear similar witness to the caste dogmas of the High Church group: "Everywhere we see the clergy, with a few persecuted exceptions (like Dr. Arnold) proclaiming themselves the advocates of Toryism, the dogged opponents of our political liberty, living either by the accursed system of pew-rents, or else by one which depends on the high price of corn; chosen exclusively from the classes who crush us down; prohibiting all free discussion on religious matters; commanding us to swallow down, with faith as passive and implicit as that of a Papist, the very creeds from which

[25] IX.
[26] I, ii, 13.
[27] XVII, 195.
[28] *Apologia,* 1865 ed. Note A, p. 501 of Ward ed.

their own bad example . . . have . . . alienated us. . . ."[29] "Soup and flannel and medicated port wine were to be had at the rectory, provided the suppliants were regular at the Sunday services, and did not dishonour the Lenten observances, and sent their children to the schools, and dropped proper curtsies, or touched their hats in all humility when his reverence and 'my lady' were encountered."[30]

The Toryism of the Puseyites is revealed by a widespread belief in the Divine Right of Kings, and a devotion to the memory of Charles I. Gresley says that English history should be taught because it inculcates the value of strictly hereditary succession. "And the disastrous consequences of popular rebellion are best learnt from a knowledge of the barbarities and crimes which took place when the dissenters rebelled against their lawful soverign, Charles I. History has also a great power to enlarge the mind. . . ."[31] In *Clement Walton* he says, "A rebellious people are always in the wrong; they disobey the commandments of God, . . . *the wrongfulness of rulers does not excuse the people's sin.*"[32] A reference to Charles I follows. Mant, in *The Village Choristers* (1854), says of the clergyman instructing the people about saints, "Nor did he forget the martyred Charles, holiest and most blessed, in that his sufferings were indeed a reflection, faint though it be and feeble, of the agony of Him, the King of Saints, Who was dragged by His own people to a death of agony and shame, His last moments embittered by the curses, and insults, and foul spittings of those whom He died to redeem, and for whose forgiveness

[29] Kingsley, *Alton Locke* (1850), II, xx, 45. Alton himself speaking.
[30] Worboise, *Overdale*, 1869, II, 19. See also *Trevor* (anon.), VIII.
[31] *Church-Clavering*, IX, 80. See also Yonge, *The Heir of Redclyffe*, V, 59, and the attack on liberal propositions by Newman quoted above.
[32] XVI, 177.

He prayed in His last moments, as did our own royal martyr for his guilty people."[33]

Indeed, the extreme Tory in politics and the extreme Catholic in religion have much in common. Both are obedient to tradition even when it involves personal sacrifice, both consider the wisdom of the Past superior to the wisdom of the latest hour, and place the law of the institution above the desire or even the judgment of the individual. Both Catholicism and the social system admired by the Tory, when they reached their greatest power, in the Middle Ages, involved a hierarchical organization headed by one man to whom was due unquestioning loyalty. Because of this, and because both are old in the experience of dealing with men, both give great emphasis to personality, more so than does the rule of majorities or of reason or of business. Both, therefore, appeal to the imagination and are intrinsically romantic. As to the Catholic only Catholics are Christian, so to the Tory only traditionalists are gentlemen. But both wear their intolerance with charming grace, for it needs no constant defense. Protected by institutional intolerance and class snobbery, the individual Tory or Catholic is often less intolerant or snobbish than the Liberal. For both Tory and Catholic there is a certain correct form for doing things, and life is surrounded by ritual, style, conventions, a grace that is old and permanent. Neither is very sharp against worldliness. Trollope's High-Church-and-Tory Lady Lufton "liked cheerful, quiet, well-to-do people, who loved their Church, their country, and their Queen, and who were not too anxious to make a noise in the world."[34] This quiet decency is characteristic.

In opposition have been, for centuries, the sects and spirit of

[33] IV, 46.
[34] *Framley Parsonage,* II, 13.

Dissent, with adherents chiefly in the middle classes. "English Liberty" is largely a product of this tradition. To a High taste, it seems very vulgar to demand individual liberty in matters of politics, religion, and social customs. Disraeli's Lord Monmouth says to Coningsby, "You go with your family, sir, like a gentleman; you are not to consider your opinions like a philosopher or a political adventurer."[35] Endymion says, "The Liberal party rather depends on the Low Church."[36] In Skene's *S. Albans* (1853), the Anglo-Catholic vicar has found the middle classes very hard to reach.[37] When a bourgeois refuses to obey hereditary authorities, or accept as God-given the place into which he is born, he lays himself open to attack as a Protestant exhibiting proud self-will. Newman wrote in a letter in 1841 that "the more serious thinkers among us are used . . . to regard the spirit of Liberalism as the characteristic of the destined Antichrist. . . . The spirit of lawlessness came in with the Reformation, and Liberalism is its offspring."[38]

Consciously opposed to the movements which characterized the nineteenth century—science, democracy, religious liberalism, and both forms of radical economics (that of laissez-faire and that of socialism)—the early Oxford Movement contributed a great deal to the process of sanctifying social prejudices. It attempted to resist the rise of the middle class by demanding obedience to the clergy, respect for the rich, and—more care for the poor. At this stage it was little less than Catholicism to the Rescue, to save England by a return to monastic almsgiving and the benevolent despotism of feudal superiors. As yet deference to the wealthy was more important than the rights of the miserable multitudes. But here lay the seeds of the future,

---

[35] *Coningsby*, III, book VIII, iii, 217.
[36] *Endymion* (1880), II, xviii, 185.
[37] *S. Albans*, V, 99-100.
[38] *Apologia*, Ch. IV, p. 284.

not even then completely ignored by the leaders of the Movement. In the war on the Middle Class and Liberalism, the old
order discovered a potentially very powerful class underneath.
Why not an alliance between the proletariat and the aristocracy, between the masses and the Church? Newman, as early
as 1833, had confessed that, "Tory as I still am theoretically
and historically, I begin to be a Radical practically."[39] The distance the Tractarians had moved from the old lazy days is
shown when the rector in Heygate's *William Blake* (1848),
wants "to show my parishioners that their clergyman is not like
a 'squire, but a real hard-working, hard-living man."[40] In *The
Parish Rescued,* by the Evangelical Wilkinson, the Tractarian
cleryman's attempt to make life pleasanter for the poor is
stigmatized as "shallow flirtation with the lower orders."[41]
This Tory Radicalism, this conception of society as organic,
divided into classes, each with its duties and rights, was best
expressed by Disraeli.

[39] *Letters and Correspondence,* I, 450 (to Rogers). In a letter to Wilson,
Sept. 8, 1833, he says, "the people were the fulcrum of the Church's power
. . . Therefore, expect on your return to England to see us all cautious,
long-headed, unfeeling, unflinching Radicals." (*Letters and Correspondence,*
I, 454.)
[40] VI, 61.
[41] III, 57.

CHAPTER V

DISRAELI: "YOUNG ENGLAND" IN RELIGION

DISRAELI differs from some of the novelists I have discussed in that he possessed the power of thought,—by no means an essential faculty in a minor novelist. In a novelist setting out to deal with intellectual systems, however, it is a permissible luxury. It enables him to offer theories of his own, which he is very likely to understand, instead of merely dramatizing the ideas of other men obscurely. Moreover, Disraeli had an additional advantage. He was religious. No nineteenth-century author, not even Newman, seemed to have a more real consciousness of Jehovah. We may read through most of the "religious" novels of the period without ever being reminded of the tone of the Bible (though footnote references to that source of law abound), but upon opening a novel by "Dizzy" the realization soon strikes us that here is the Semitic mind which has created three religions. For neither Milton nor Carlyle, with all their prophetic power, are so Hebraic in spirit as this wit and politician. Indeed, it seems to be Disraeli's unquestioning whole-souled belief that permits him his bold play of intellect and fancy over religious questions. What other orthodox foe of the scientists would have dared write, "It is not good taste to believe in the Devil. Give me a single argument against his personality which is not applicable to the personality of the Deity."[1] Disraeli does not

---

[1] *Endymion*, II, xviii, 188.

seem to have considered his religion a fragile thing. By contrast, he contributes to the conviction that the lack of ruddy cheer in Victorian faith is evidence of doubt gnawing at the core. But if Anglo-Saxons are not able to utter pure Hebraism, they have always received it with unusual sympathy. Likewise, no Englishman has ever been able to put into words so convincing a plea for English Toryism as Disraeli—a plea too logical to be truly British. Whether we consider the Oxford Movement in its religious or its social aspect, we find Disraeli's New Toryism (called "Young Englandism"), running parallel. Indeed, the two are classed together in *Trevor*,[2] in Wilkinson's *The Parish Rescued*,[3] and in *Ridley Seldon*,[4] by Anne Howard.

In Disraeli's *Contarini Fleming* (1832), the hero becomes a Catholic because of the sensuous beauty of that worship.[5] (But this was written before the Anglo-Catholic revival began.) Disraeli said that he entirely participated at the time in the feeling that influenced the Oxford Movement, and thought that it could have conquered the nation.[6] He seems to have imbibed his first serious interest in the Church from the Cambridge men who, in 1841, formed his Young England party.[7] He wrote a trilogy of novels, *Coningsby* (1844), *Sybil* (1845) and *Tancred* (1847) on the three topics, respectively, of the political, economic, and religious regeneration of England. But in the first he launched all three, including "the duties of

[2] VIII.
[3] VII, 156.
[4] VII, 78, "old Protestant England—threatening to change her name, and her faith, and to call herself 'Young England,' Anglo-Catholic England, Unprotestant England."
[5] I, part I, xii, 117.
[6] Monypenny and Buckle, *Life of Benjamin Disraeli*, IV, 350.
[7] Monypenny and Buckle, *op. cit.*, IV, 351.

the Church as a main remedial agent."[8] Coningsby, the hero, grew convinced that something fervent and well-defined should be substituted for latitudinarianism.[9] We are told that the Church is the estate of the People, the medium by which the despised and degraded classes assert the native equality of man.[10]

Sybil (1845) deals with the economic condition of the people. Disraeli sees Catholicism as a popular institution in its economics. The original purpose of the church estates was "the education of the people and the maintenance of the poor."[11] "Were there any rick-burners in the times of the lord abbots? And if not, why not?"[12] The Monastics, we are told, were easy landlords. The monks were sons of the people. "As long as the monks existed, the people, when aggrieved, had property on their side."[13] The priest and the gentleman were "the ancient champions of the people against arbitrary courts and rapacious parliaments."[14] But the Church has deserted the people.[15]

It is the third novel of the trilogy, *Tancred; or The New Crusade* (1847), which is devoted to the problem of the Church. This is the story of a young English nobleman, who goes to Palestine to seek religious inspiration at its source. Tancred contrasts Occidental and Semitic society, and thinks of his dissatisfaction with the former, "his conviction of the growing melancholy of enlightened Europe," veiled as it may

[8] Disraeli, "General Preface" to 1870 ed. of Novels, p. xii.
[9] I, book III, ii, 266.
[10] III, VII, ii, 108.
[11] I, I, iii, 23.
[12] I, II, iv, 135.
[13] I, II, v, 140-144.
[14] II, IV, xv, 312.
[15] I, II, xii, 253.

be under conceited bustle, shipwreck gaiety, or the empiricism of science.[16] On Mount Sinai, he prays, "Why no longer do the messages of thy renovating will descend on earth? Faith fades and duty dies. A profound melancholy has fallen on the spirit of man. The priest doubts, the monarch cannot rule, the multitude moans and toils. . . ." He sees a vision of the angel of Arabia, who tells him that Europe is again in the throes of a great birth. "The multitudes again are brooding; but they are not now in the forests; they are in the cities and in the fertile plains. Since the first sun of this century rose, the intellectual colony of Arabia, once called Christendom, has been in a state of partial and blind revolt. Discontented, they attributed their suffering to the principles to which they owed all their happiness, and in receding from which they had become proportionately miserable. . . . Cease, then, to seek in a vain philosophy the solution of the social problem that perplexes you. Announce the sublime and solacing doctrine of theocratic equality."[17] Finally, according to the Queen of the Ansarey, the time has arisen for Asia to reassert its supremacy in the realm of ideas. Syria and Arabia united should conquer the world. "We wish to conquer that world, with angels at our head, in order that we may establish the happiness of man by a divine dominion, and, crushing the political atheism that is now desolating existence, utterly extinguish the grovelling tyranny of self-government."[18] Though a High Church Anglican, Disraeli also emphasizes frequently the divine mission of the Semitic peoples. In his "General Preface" to the 1870 edition of his novels, he says that there must be occasional jealous discontent with the Revelation entrusted a particular race. "But there is no reason to believe that the

[16] II, IV, iv, 204.
[17] II, IV, vii, 242-246.
[18] III, VI, iii, 165.

Teutonic rebellion of this century against the Divine truths entrusted to the Semites will ultimately meet with more success than the Celtic insurrection of the preceding age."[19] (It is sad that he could not have added "or the Slavic revolt of the twentieth century.")

Most of the Tractarians oppose scepticism on the grounds of faith, Disraeli on the grounds of conviction. The former are more dogmatic, and say obediently, "What is it my duty to believe?" The latter is more mystical, or, rather, more incapable of the sceptical mood, and merely states his belief. Instead of appealing to scriptural texts and ecclesiastical history, Disraeli speaks direct, as do Bibles, to the intuition of the reader. It would not be just to see in this an inferiority as to religious insight for the Catholic belief, since Disraeli is obviously a greater genius than our other Anglo-Catholic novelists, and in Newman we shall again find what might be called religious experience at first hand (though still a moral element enters into the test of evidence). The interesting thing about Disraeli is that it does not seem to be experience that speaks, but inborn consciousness, as if this Jew had the Law in his heart;—there is the same difference between European Christianity (or European irreligion) and the Bible: the Bible does not argue. But, though Disraeli and the Tractarians are at points as far apart as Judaism and Catholicism, they often move side by side. And in the broader sense that the Oxford Movement is a reaction against intellectual and political liberalism, a revival of the desire for supernatural grace granted through a human society that especially represents God (rather than through individual faith or reason), they are both in the same current of radical reaction.

But with the secession of Newman, Disraeli lost hope in the

[19] P. xvi, Cf. also *Sybil*, I, II, xii, 255; Monypenny and Buckle, *op. cit.*, IV, 350.

Oxford Movement itself,[20] and the agitation over the Papal Aggression convinced him that the religion for England must be Protestant.[21] Of the second stage of the Anglo-Catholic revival, Ritualism, he was the avowed foe, calling it "Mass in masquerade."[22] In 1870, looking back on the early Oxford Movement, he says that if a churchman equal to the occasion had then arisen, the Church might have been an important factor in building up a stable society. "But these great matters fell into the hands of monks and schoolmen;" and Newman's secession dealt a blow under which the Church of England still reels.[23]

Monypenny sees the Oxford Movement as one of the indirect causes of Disraeli's Toryism.[24] I have shown reason to think the early Oxford Movement was, largely, the religious side of a movement that was Tory on its social side. I should hesitate to call either a cause of the other, in any fundamental sense. Of course, there was close interaction between these two branches of reaction, but they were both manifestations of the same spirit, already found together in Scott.[25] Monypenny's account of the "Young England" Tories would, by a mere

[20] Monypenny and Buckle, *op. cit.* IV, 350-351.

[21] *Ibid.* III, 271.

[22] Speech in the House of Commons, July 15, 1874. Hansard, *Parliamentary Debates,* Third Series, vol. CCXXI, p. 80.

[23] "General Preface," pp. xiv, xv.

[24] *Op. cit.,* II, 170-171.

[25] Cf. *Fraser's Magazine,* XXXVI (1847), 351: "From taking Scott as our guide and instructor, we are learning to prefer to patient thought and candid investigation, an easily-induced attention to the imaginary graces and prettiness of the past,—

'Le donne, i cavalier, l'ame, gli amori,

Le cortesie, l'audaci impresse,'

and the consequence is that Mr. Smythe is likely to be the exponent of our opinions in History, Mr. Pugin of our views of Religion, and Lord John Manners of our statesmanship."

change of names, read like an account of the rise of Tractarianism: On the Tory side in the Parliament of 1841, there was a group of young men educated together at Cambridge, led by George Smythe, original of the hero in *Coningsby* and Waldershare in *Endymion*. They were Romantics when Romanticism was now not revolutionary but reactionary. Their Toryism never lost a certain Jacobite flavour. The Oxford Movement gave a seventeenth-century colour to their political ideas, and they were strongly influenced by admiration for Laud and Stafford. They turned their backs on the degenerate Toryism of privilege and immobility (compare the attitude of the Tractarians towards the High and Dry), and they desired for the Church greater independence. Feeling an antipathy to the middle classes, they wished to provide a counterpoise by reawakening a sense of duty in the nobility and gentry. But they also had faith in the lower orders. Smythe and his friends began to rally around Disraeli. No party bound by formal pledges seems to have been formed. But, in 1843, they were recognized as a coterie and known as "Young England." They had faith in Toryism, conviction of the possibility of restoring it to vigor by reconstructing it on a popular basis, a desire to strengthen the influence of the upper orders, a readiness to trust the masses (with a genuine interest in their well-being) and a dislike of Liberalism.[26] Only a reconstructed Tory party, according to Disraeli, could infuse life and vigour into the Church as trainer of the nation, and "emancipate the political constituency of 1832 from its sectarian bondage and contracted sympathies . . . and all this rather by the use of ancient forms and the restoration of the past than by political revolutions founded on abstract ideas."[27]

[26] Monypenny and Buckle, *op. cit.*, II, 162ff.
[27] "General Preface," pp. x, xi.

Disraeli's *Coningsby* was regarded as the manifesto of Young England.[28]

Liberalism is founded on abstract ideas, and its opposite is more personal. Hence, the party which attacks "popular rights" is often the most popular party, and the church which asks most submission from the people seems to have fixed itself most firmly in their hearts. Disraeli was a real Tory in assuming that nations are motivated not by a desire for equality, liberty, or even economic welfare, but by enthusiastic faiths and stirring loyalties.[29] He was also a true Tory in wishing to follow traditions distinctly *national.* He believed that the English have always been Catholic, though even in the Middle Ages anti-papal.[30] Like many Anglo-Catholic novelists, he tended to look upon Victorian life as if it were Medieval. His *Tancred* has for a subtitle *The New Crusade,* and it is the story of how a pure young nobleman goes on a religious quest to Palestine,—in the nineteenth century. *Sybil,* his study of the results of the industrial revolution in England, in places as radical as Upton Sinclair, is yet permeated with aristocratic feeling, and the happy ending is achieved by making the hero and heroine inherit a title. The people, whose misery the book reveals, are to be saved from above, and can be led only by aristocrats, "the natural leaders of the People" and "the only ones."[31] One character says, "I was a Franklin's son myself" but "it is the serfs I live among of whom I am thinking."[32] Mr. St. Lys, a Tractarian priest, is called "a fine gentleman-saint."[33] (It would be hard to find a better phrase to describe the ideal hero presented in the Anglo-Catholic fiction of the

[28] Monypenny and Buckle, *op. cit.,* II, 199.
[29] E.g. *Coningsby,* II, IV, xiii, 177-178.
[30] *Sybil,* I, I, iii, 46.
[31] II, bk. IV, xv, 318 (The hero speaking, for Disraeli).
[32] I, bk. II, xvi, 313.
[33] II, III, ii, 25.

nineteenth century.) In *Endymion* (1880), Disraeli was to describe a tournament—based on one which actually took place in 1839 at Eglinton castle.[34]

Disraeli wrote no novels between *Tancred,* 1847, and *Lothair,* completed in 1870. Thus he wrote fiction in two controversial decades, but not in the lull between them. This chapter has been concerned with the early Disraeli, enemy of liberalism. In technique, his novels of the 'forties are similar to contemporary Anglo-Catholic fiction, with the curious modification that a very wise Jew often appears to solve some difficulty. As in other controversial novels of the decade, the story is a vehicle for the presentation of argument, and the love interest is entirely subordinate. They are novels of adventure in the realm of ideas.

Disraeli did great things in England, and he gave to Toryism a philosophy acceptable to the reason—which is perhaps an irrelevancy. Through his Oriental power of creating aphorism, he probably helped to sharpen English wit into the brilliance of Wilde and Shaw. But he did not "belong" (in an esthetic sense) to Victorian England. His career was like an incident from the Arabian Nights incongruously set in "an insular country subject to fogs, and with a powerful middle class." He was very like Anglo-Catholicism itself,—a spirit of Semitic origin adapting itself to rule England in the shape of an English gentleman, but by the really conservative British of the time looked upon as something fundamentally foreign. And yet, for all they opposed the modern spirit, Disraeli's system and Catholicism itself are fresh and challenging today, when many a set of Victorian ideas once new seem as old-fashioned, dull, and artificial as a bustle.

[34] II, xxiii, 232. See Escott, T.H.S., *Social Transformations of the Victorian Age,* 3.

CHAPTER VI

NEWMAN AS NOVELIST

JOHN HENRY NEWMAN wrote two novels, both portraying a development of mind somewhat similar to his
own,—a development which, for him, culminated in one
of the most important events in the history of the Church
since the Reformation, his conversion to Rome. Since fiction
is freer than history, some of Newman's spiritual experiences
are suggested here that are not set forth in the *Apologia*.
Loss and Gain appeared in 1848, only three years after his
conversion, and it reflects immediately the Oxford phase of the
Movement. In the summer of 1847, some tale directed against
the converts to the Catholic faith had been sent to Newman.
"Its contents were as wantonly and preposterously fanciful,
as they were injurious to those whose motives and actions it
professed to represent; but a formal criticism . . . seemed . . .
out of place. The suitable answer lay rather in the publication of a second tale; drawn up with a stricter regard to truth
and probability, and with at least some personal knowledge
of Oxford, and some perception of the various aspects of the
religious phenomenon, which the work in question handled so
rudely and unskilfully."[1] The result was *Loss and Gain: The
Story of a Convert*, a realistic novel of contemporary life in
form largely argumentative dialogue. It is austerely barren
of the pleasures of plot. Charles Reding, son of an old-fashioned clergyman of the Church of England, goes to Oxford

[1] Advertisement to the Sixth Edition, 1874, p. ix.

(54)

and becomes interested in Catholicism. Suspected of being more Roman than is strictly true at the time, he is sent home from college. Because of the distractions of religious uncertainity, he fails in the examination for honours. He even postpones taking his B.A. because of conscientious difficulties in subscribing to the Articles. The conviction that Rome is the only true Church grows on him. At last, after various sects try to win him, he joins the Church of Rome.

In the early spring of the same year that *Loss and Gain* was published, Newman also began what was to become the sub-plot of *Callista: A Sketch of the Third Century*, writing then parts of chapters I, IV, and V, and sketching the character and fortunes of Juba.[2] A year later, in a letter of February 28, 1849, he says, speaking of historical work:

> What I should like would be to bring out the ἦθος of the Heathen from St. Paul's day down to St. Gregory, when under the process, or in the sight of the phenomenon, of conversion; what conversion *was* in those times, and what the position of a Christian in that world of sin, what the sophistries of philosophy viewed as realities influencing men. But besides the great difficulty of finding time, I don't think I could do it from History. I despair of finding facts enough—as if an imaginary tale could alone embody the conclusions to which existing facts *lead*.[3]

Evidently the general idea of what became the main plot of *Callista* was beginning to take shape in his mind. He did nothing more with this story for six years. In July, 1855, he suddenly resumed it and completed it in a few months.[4] It appeared in 1856. Kingsley's *Hypatia*, published three years before, had offended the more Catholic party in the Church of England with its tolerance of pagan thought and its attack

---

[2] Postscript (after Advertisement), pp. vii-viii.
[3] Letter to Frederick Capes, quoted in Ward, *Life of . . . Newman*, I, 245.
[4] Postscript, *Callista*, p. viii.

on monasticism among the early Christians.[5] The purpose of Newman's novel is the opposite, that is, "to imagine and express, from a Catholic point of view, the feelings and mutual relations of Christians and heathens at the period to which it belongs."[6] This, too, is a story of conversion, and hence its basis in the author's own experience lay in the period when he was yet an Anglican. It is something of a historical romance, something of a saint's life, something of a psychological study, and, though less so than *Loss and Gain*, something of a series of arguments. Agellius, a Christian, loves Callista, a Greek girl who works for his uncle. Though a pagan, she is interested in hearing about Christianity. Since a plague of locusts is ascribed to the presence of the Christians, a mob rises against them. In its wild fury it captures Callista at the hut of Agellius. In prison, she finally joins the Church, and becomes a martyr and saint. Her body works miracles, for instance curing of his madness Juba, brother of Agellius, who had been under the evil influence of their mother, the witch Gurta.

Although the advertisement of 1848 states specifically that *Loss and Gain* is not the history of any individual mind among the recent converts,[7] we now know enough of Newman's life to show that he has drawn largely upon his own experience, even to many details. The hero, like the author, was retiring and over-sensitive, and in his first years at college he was much alone.[8] Like Newman, he stood for honours and failed.[9] Mr. Reilley points out that both were impatient of party men and "mere talkers," expressed a love of Gregorian music, and that

[5] *Charles Kingsley, His Letters and Memories of his Life*, ed. by his wife, I, 366; II, 179.
[6] *Callista*, Advertisement, p. vii.
[7] P. vii.
[8] *Loss and Gain*, Part I, Ch. i, p. 3; *Apologia*, Ch. I, 118.
[9] *Loss and Gain*, II, xxi, 335; *Letters and Correspondence*, I, 46.

"the 'Father Dominic', a Passionist born in Italy, who received Reding into the Church, was the same" in name and antecedents as he who received Newman himself.[10] We may add that both felt from boyhood that they should remain celibate.[11] Both delayed their entrance into the Catholic Church for a long time to be sure that they were not deluded. And Reding's estrangement from Sheffield is paralleled by Newman's from Frederic Rogers, long his most intimate friend. Like Reding and Sheffield, they had roomed on the same staircase at Oxford.[12] On the other hand, it seems to have been an event in the life of another, a Mr. Morris, that suggested the incident in which Charles is sent home from college because of coming into conflict with his college authority over his belief in the Intercession of the Saints. Like Mr. Morris, Reding in the novel draws a distinction between Intercession and Invocation.[13] But Reding is not Newman, and the Oxford Movement in which he is taking part has been sketched with the central figure omitted. There is a passing reference to the preaching at St. Mary's,[14] but we miss entirely the politics, parties, combat, leadership, action of corporate bodies, and attempts to influence public opinion, which are part of the Movement. The author's gaze is turned inward upon the development of an individual soul.

As we might expect from so skillful a controversialist as Newman, his novels are largely devoted to presenting Catholic

[10] Reilley, J. J., *Newman as a Man of Letters,* 82.

[11] *Apologia,* I, 110-111; *Loss and Gain,* II, iv, 192; Cf. also III, ii, 349, a passage of which a Freudian might make much.

[12] Thureau-Dangin, *op. cit.,* I, 262-263.

[13] *Loss and Gain,* II, x, 234-241; *Correspondence of John Henry Newman with John Keble and Others,* 229-230.

[14] *Loss and Gain,* II, iii, 184; see also *Correspondence . . . with John Keble and Others,* 200-201 where "Smith" of *Loss and Gain,* II, 120, is associated with Newman.

doctrines and portraying Catholic practices. That he wished
some of the discussions in *Loss and Gain* to be received as
serious explanations of his views is indicated by a passage in
a letter written thirty-one years later: "And now I go on to
the relation of the will to assent . . . as to which . . . I have not
made my doctrine quite clear to you in the passage in Loss
and Gain."[15] He then analyzes in detail the passage in question. Sometimes Newman embodies his ideas in concrete events.
Baptism suddenly produced in Callista a serenity different
from anything she had ever before the power of conceiving.[16]
But more often he pushes the story aside and presents his
arguments directly, putting them into the mouth of a figure
who seldom exists as anything more than a mouth from which
comes forth theory. Occasionally he rejects even this ghost of
narrative and speaks out from the page *in propria persona,*—
as when he opens a chapter by arguing that, "There is no
. . . inconsistency in a person first using his private judgment
[to reach Catholicism] and then denouncing its use,"[17] or when
he defends dogma by saying that unless there is one center on
which the mind sits men will be inconsistent, but real liberty
consists in being subject to truth.[18] Now that Newman has
left the Anglican Church, it is interesting to see how he answers the thesis of his own Tract 90, which caused the series
to be stopped: The argument is that the Articles may be given
a Catholic interpretation. Charles' reply is that the English
Church *might* have adopted this interpretation, but did not.[19]

[15] Unfinished letter to William Froude, Rome, April 29, 1879, quoted in
Ward, *Life of . . . Newman,* Appendices, II, p. 591.
[16] *Callista,* XXXI, 348.
[17] *Loss and Gain,* II, vi.
[18] *Ibid.,* I, iii, 17-18.
[19] *Ibid.,* I, xv, 132-135.

Among the other subjects dealt with in the novels are the Apostolic Succession, Mass, Vestments, Confession, the Supremacy of Rome, Devotion to the Blessed Virgin.

Newman's chief opponent, Kingsley, preaching a Christianity that considered physical well-being a valuable aid to a Christian life, had prefaced *Hypatia* with an attack on asceticism. Newman takes the other side. When Callista's health is injured by the heat of the prison and she loses her former beauty, he tells us that rudiments of a diviner loveliness were taking its place.[20] And Charles Reding says, "the idea of an apostle, unmarried, pure, in fast and nakedness, at length a martyr, is a higher idea than that of one of the old Israelites sitting under his vine and fig-tree, full of temporal goods, and surrounded by sons and grandsons."[21] Charles says he fancied that fasting, abstinence, and celibacy might be taken as a make-up for sin.[22] When Callista asked to be made a Christian, there was an "utter disappearance of that majesty of mien . . . a gift, so beautiful, so unsuitable to fallen man. . . . She had lost every vestige of what the world worships under the titles of proper pride and self-respect."[23] Proud liberty of intellect is denounced. We are shown the fate of Juba, brother of the hero, who, for his free-thinking, is punished with madness, being possessed with an evil spirit. Against his will, Juba falls on his knees before an idol of Pan, laps up the blood of sacrifice, and among other horrible things spouts a chorus of Greek, a language he had never heard before.[24] But even while yet a maniac, he has changed for the better, we are told, for his

[20] *Callista*, XXVIII, 307-308.
[21] *Loss and Gain*, II, v, 196-197.
[22] *Ibid.*, II, v, 200.
[23] *Callista*, XXXI, 345.
[24] *Ibid.*, XXIV, 271.

expression of pride is gone.[25] The sign of the cross he cannot resist in spite of manifest antagonism. At last, after Callista's death, he is forced to touch the feet of her corpse. The evil spirit goes out, leaving him an idiot.[26] Newman's direct argument for belief in miracles is much more plausible than this concrete illustration.[27] But this part of the tale is one of the most interesting of the Catholic attacks upon the scepticism of Victorian science, and one of the strangest fruits of a strange imagination. The nineteenth century, for all its Medievalizing, seldom came nearer to producing something that might really have been written during the Middle Ages, for this incident is surrounded with no atmosphere of romantic distance. And whatever the faults of Newman as an historical novelist, we cannot accuse him of being out of sympathy with his subject. Indeed, his mind preferred to dwell in centuries earlier than the Medieval. It was to the writers of the first Christian centuries that he went for guidance. "The Fathers," he said, "made me a Catholic."[28] Indeed, he himself seems to belong with the early Christians. Was not the decaying empire of pagan culture destroyed by just such penetrating dogmatism and subtle patience, sacrificing every measurable and worldly good, nay, even every liberty of the private judgment, in grim obedience to an intuition of God? I suspect that modern scepticism does not fully know the deep strength of its foe, this power of faith, that it has taken up weapons against so lightly.

The problem of the relation between an author's religious convictions and his artistic technique has been somewhat neglected by literary scholarship. We have in Newman ex-

---

[25] *Ibid.*, XXXI, 349.
[26] *Ibid.*, XXXVI, 380-381.
[27] See *Apologia,* Note B, p. 401.
[28] Newman, *Certain Difficulties felt by Anglicans,* 24.

cellent examples of this connection. His belief in miracles permits him to use, with serious intent, certain devices which, in
some writers, would seem merely unreal coincidence or romantic accident. He tells us that the plague of locusts was sent
from God because of the iniquity of the inhabitants of Sicca.
The "natural and direct interpretation was, 'Do penance, and
be converted.' "[29] We have already mentioned how he disposes
of the arguments of scepticism by delivering the sceptic to an
evil spirit. But, in spite of this and other colorful materials in
the historical romance, a certain tepidness of treatment keeps
it from giving the delight expected. His heart was not in this
sort of thing. Who was he to set himself telling of narrow
escapes and love affairs, or describing the appearance of a mob
or of a witch—this austere mystic? He had no interest in the
externals of things. "I wish I lived as much in the unseen
world," he said, "as I think I do not live in this."[30]

The plots of the two novels reflect Newman's asceticism. *Loss
and Gain* is as devoid of a love story as is any biography of its
author. To the conversion story of his later romance, he adds
the fact that Agellius is in love with Callista. That is as far
as it goes. When she, not yet a Christian, rebukes her lover
for courting her instead of trying to convert her, he is shocked
at his own conduct and bitterly repentant.[31] The novel ends
not in a marriage but in death. All the emotional ecstasy that
would ordinarily be lavished upon sexual love is devoted to
the divine. As Callista was put on the rack, "She spoke her

[29] *Callista*, XVI, 178-179. Cf. the way the Anglo-Catholic novelist William
Sewell kills off a Jesuitical-Chartist villain in *Hawkstone*, II, xxiii, 337:
"It was an accident—such an accident as Providence usually employs in
executing his justest vengeance!"

[30] *Letters and Correspondence*, II, 279.

[31] *Callista*, XI, XII.

last word, 'For Thee, my Lord and Love, for Thee!... Accept me, O my Love, upon this bed of pain! And come to me, O my Love, make haste and come!' "[32] When Chione (the slave), and Agellius spoke of their Master, they blushed.[33]

If the author does not succeed in giving us the thrill of adventure and the feeling of a colorful historical background in *Callista*, nor the political aspect of the Oxford Movement in *Loss and Gain*, it must be remembered that in both novels Newman is chiefly interested in the inner drama of a change in faith. The belief that the most important event in life is not any measurable success nor even human failure, but the attainment of a certain subjective attitude, assent, communion with the true Church, this belief makes itself manifest in the choice of incident and the management of each story, and is present in the climax. This concentration upon one character and one action gives excellent unity of structure. On the other hand, it does permit *dialogue* that is quite undramatic, that reflects merely intellectual steps along the way to conversion, not emotional reaction of man on man.

But the most important influence of Newman's religious beliefs upon his technique grows out of his conviction that the progress of a soul is ultimately not due to its surroundings nor to the individual himself, but to God.[34] The novel of Hardy and of Zola, under the sway of "scientific" determinism, was to become a study of the influence of environment upon character. Newman in each of his novels gives us a plot based upon the opposite assumption, a picture of a character acting in a certain way *in spite of* heredity, environment, and self-interest. He considered his own conversion the result of a call, or "an

[32] *Ibid.*, XXXIV, 369.
[33] *Ibid.*, XIX, 221.
[34] *Ibid.*, XIX, 223; *Loss and Gain*, II, vi, 204-205.

election of grace."[35] Before coming to his final decision, he
had held aloof from Roman Catholics. Similarly, the hero in
Loss and Gain, up to the time when he decides he must join
their Church, does not know any Roman Catholics.[36] It is not
even the writings of the early Fathers which make Reding a
Catholic, as it was in Newman's own case. In the *Apologia,* the
author has told us what books caused him to doubt the validity
of Anglicanism. But doubt occurs to Charles without such
preparation.[37] Charles, we are told, could not escape the destiny
of being one of the elect of God.[38] A naturalistic novel, as a
study in mundane cause and effect, makes the background a
part of the story, almost one of the actors, that could not be
removed without breaking a link in the sequence of events.
Newman's supernaturalism allows him to write without achieving that intimate fusion of setting and plot. We feel that the
subjective study has been worked out first, then the frame
fitted rather awkwardly around it. The social and physical
world never emerges into convincing reality. In his youth,
Newman had "thought life might be a dream, or I an Angel,
and all this world a deception, my fellow-angels by a playful
device concealing themselves from me, and deceiving me with
the semblance of a material world."[39] In his novels, action and
setting are hardly more than coating for the pill. He seems to
pull up his conversion-story at certain intervals, as if to say,
"Now I must stop the argument and describe the scenery or
let the characters drink another cup of tea."

It is interesting to compare Newman to Eliot, who, chrono-

[35] See letter quoted by W. S. Lilly in "Anglicanism Old and New,"
Dublin Review, CXXXVIII, Jan. 1906, p. 174. Cf. *Apologia* I, 110.
[36] III, v, 370; and III, ix, 417.
[37] *Loss and Gain,* I, xi, 92.
[38] That is, of becoming a Catholic. *Ibid.,* II, vi, 206.
[39] *Apologia,* I, 106.

logically and philosophically, lies between him and the naturalists. Her position is not merely that of determinism.[40] Protestant in her origins, she emphasizes the moral responsibility of
the individual. She attempts to penetrate to the ultimate motives that cause the will to swerve from duty, and soberly analyzes the consequences of deeds. Newman, vividly conscious of
being in the hand of God, shows us not the consequences of
acts of will, but the stages in the path along which the soul is
led by a divine power quite independent of time, place, circum-
stance, and personal inclination. Of course, this is not to say that
Newman denies free will. It is open to the soul to decide for itself whether it will or will not follow the light which God has
granted, but the important thing is the act of grace, not the act
of will. Newman's chief characters do not exhibit a conflict of
desire and duty. They are eager to obey if only they may learn
what is right. They are full of hope, for nothing can prevent the
interposition of a personal Deity, actually a *deus ex machina*.
There is no real conflict, no real suspense, in these plots. From
the first, we can see what is coming. And yet we miss the feeling of inevitability which an irresistible impersonal cause or
Fate would give us.

In short, with the novel of psychological study, as we pass
from Newman through Eliot to Hardy we pass from supernaturalism, in which a man's fate is offered him by benevolent
Providence; through a form of moral Protestantism in which
men owe their fate largely to their own actions, and then to
Naturalism, in which fate is determined by circumstances.
Hence the setting was to become more and more important.
Trollope and Eliot, writing later than Newman, gave with
artistic care the local color that would be perceived by the

[40] Cf. Letters to the Hon. Mrs. Ponsonby, Dec. 10, 1874, and Aug. 19,
1875, in J. W. Cross, *George Eliot's Life*, III, 176f. and 188f.

normal human consciousness, not yet the background as discovered by the mystic or scientist. But with Egdon Heath, of *The Return of the Native,* or the social milieu of Zola's *Débâcle,* the setting becomes the real center of interest. Second only to background for increasing importance is the past of the individual; in Eliot, Trollope, (and Yonge), the individual's earlier deeds; in Hardy even his heredity.

The divine influence which guides Callista is not merely conscience, but a voice from a Personality outside herself.[41] Nevertheless, conscience is on the side of the Creator,[42] Who has planted in us, the *Apologia* says, certain sentiments of right and wrong. Both Callista and Charles Reding seem to know what they ought to believe before they believe it, a complex psychological condition which may perhaps help us to understand Newman's own development. Callista's "was not a change which involved contrariety, but one which expanded itself in (as it were) concentric circles." Every day was the child of the preceding, yet "had she been asked . . . where was her principle and consistency, what was her logic, or whether she acted on reason, or on impulse, or on feeling, or in fancy, or in passion, she would have been reduced to silence."[43] Hence her strange rebuke, while she is yet pagan, to her lover for not preaching Christianity to her. When she first read the Gospel, she found that here was that towards which her intellect tended, though that intellect could only approve, not originate.[44] Charles Reding, having a notion that celibacy is better than married life, when he sees that Catholicism justifies his thoughts and explains his feeling, finds this a

[41] *Callista,* XXVIII, 314; cf. XXVII, 293.
[42] Cf. as to Juba, *ibid.,* XIV, 165.
[43] *Callista,* XXVII, 291-292.
[44] *Ibid.,* XXIX, 326.

direct argument for Catholicism.[45] "Conviction," says Charles, "is the eyesight of the mind, not a conclusion from premises; God works it, and His works are slow."[46] But Charles seems to know as well as his author where he is going. And so does the reader.

The creation of characters is probably the ultimate test of an author's breadth and humanity. When Newman gives us prototypes of himself, they are real enough. But if we compare his characters, say with those of the Colloquies of Erasmus (who are also figures created for the presentation of Catholic arguments), we are tempted to conclude that Newman's sympathy was confined within the bounds of his dogma. It is not that Catholic thinking itself involves meagerness of sympathy for *la perduta gente*. Newman loved to repeat that for him there were but two beings of any consequence, God and himself.[47] To those of his creatures who are neither Romanist nor High Anglican, he is absurdly unjust, seeming to assume that the lost soul knows at heart the truth of Catholic doctrine but through sinful stubbornness refuses to admit it. Juba is not only sceptical, he is also superstitious. He uses amulets against scorpions, and stands for intellectual freedom. When a priest claims him "as one of my children" Juba winces, but says scornfully, "You are mistaken there father; speak to those who own you. I am a free man."[48] Of these hostile portraits, the most interesting are those in which Newman, with cold scorn, angles a puppet to typify ridiculously some opinion he dislikes. In *Loss and Gain*, there is a cutting satire in designating the Evangelicals present at a tea as No. 1, No. 2, No. 3.[49]

[45] *Loss and Gain*, II, vi, 204-205.
[46] *Ibid.*, II, xvii, 294.
[47] Thureau-Dangin, *op. cit.*, III, 95.
[48] *Callista*, XIV, 163.
[49] I, xvii, 146-154.

But he makes most sport with the representatives of absurd cults who, just before Reding joins the Catholic Church, try to win him to their own religions. There is Dr. Kitchens with his book "Spiritual Elixer," of which the "operation is mild and pleasurable" and acts in a few hours.[50] A young lady tells him that some of them are organizing a religious body. He asks their tenets.

> "Here, too," she replied, "there is much still to be done; the tenets are not fixed either, that is, they are but sketched; and we shall prize your suggestions much. Nay, you will, of course, have the opportunity, as you would have the right, to nominate any doctrine to which you may be especially inclined."
>
> Charles did not know how to answer to so liberal an offer.[51]

Considered merely as a story, *Callista* shows a marked improvement over the earlier novel, for it has more plot, more suspense, more emotion, more action. On the other hand, *Loss and Gain,* dealing as it does with contemporary experience, leaves an impression of deeper sincerity. Its casual flow of argument, its England and its Oxford and its mild clerical life seem very near reality. But not on such an esthetic basis would Newman have us judge his books. The novelists of the 'forties had more serious purposes in mind. Anne Mozley tells us that "The ethos, as Mr. Newman calls it, of a book came always foremost in his critical estimation."[52] He writes in 1837 that he misses something in Jane Austen. "What vile creatures her parsons are! She has not a dream of the high Catholic $\check{\eta}\theta o\varsigma$."[53] And when he came to write novels himself ten years later his first concern, as I have shown, was to paint souls moved by

---

[50] *Loss and Gain,* III, viii, 409.
[51] *Ibid.,* III, vii, 396.
[52] *Letters and Correspondence,* II, 224, note 1.
[53] *Ibid.,* II, 224, Letter to Mrs. John Mozley, Jan. 19, 1837.

Catholic ideals. He was using fiction to convey dramatically moral insight into values that may make character and determine conduct. Besides esthetic and ethical interest, Newman's novels have unusual historical and biographical value. He calls *Loss and Gain* "A Tale, which . . . is a more intelligible and exact representation of the thoughts, sentiments, and aspirations . . ." prevailing then at Oxford "than was to be found in the pamphlets, charges, sermons, reviews, and story-books of the day."[54] We see what it meant to turn the back on one's family and the high wordly position of an English clergyman, to join the despised Catholics.[55] As long as men turn to literature for serious knowledge of human character, of social history, and of the ideals that have moulded conduct, these novels will always be documents of some value. I have treated them at such length because of their earnest portrayal—with a delicate insight into rare states of mind—of a profound and very important change of belief, a Protestant's conversion to Rome, by the one who, of all men with literary power in the nineteenth century, had best knowledge of that experience. These novels are built upon that portion of Newman's life which is the central fact in the history of Romanism and of Anglo-Catholicism in modern England.

[54] Dedication, p. vi.
[55] *Loss and Gain,* III, v, 370.

CHAPTER VII

THE ACHIEVEMENT OF THE 'FORTIES

IN SUMMARY, we may say that in the eighteen-forties and, in some cases, on into the early 'fifties, the novels (of whatever school of thought) which reflect the Oxford Movement are chiefly controversial—in their belligerent tone, their subordination of story to sermon, their method of constructing characters to argue, and situations to illustrate, some theory. Indeed, the writers often boast of a purpose and scorn the imputation that they are writing to amuse.[1] For the most part incredibly prosaic, these stories hug the ground as if even the warmth of religious fervor were not able to break the cocoon spun by an age of social reports, tracts, and economic conflict. The novels sometimes have either a love affair or end in a marriage, but seldom achieve both—successful loves should not occupy the mind of a Catholic priest, though a wife may be allowed to an Anglican. What love-story there is the author usually brings in reluctantly, shame-facedly, and as an aside. But, lacking romance, the novels are even naïve in their realism. Novelists of this period may insist in a preface that they are telling a True Story, with some disguise,[2] or slip in a footnote saying that this actually happened.[3] References to other authors abound. These novels may be considered the forerunners of those of the later natural-

[1] See above, first part of Chapter II, also William Sewell, *Hawkstone*, Preface to Second ed. 1845.
[2] *Steepleton; Earlswood.*
[3] E.g. *Warden of Berkingholt*, VII, 158-159.

istic school that were to embody materials collected in note-books. If not yet "scientific," they were already "documented." On the other hand, one true source of realistic effect, description, is very much neglected,—though an exception must be made here for some of the exalted rhetoric of Lady Novelists.

Throughout the 'forties, the arguments are chiefly legalistic. Too often today the Oxford Movement is thought of as the offspring of esthetic yearning. If the novels we have been discussing contributed no other item to the history of the Movement, they would justify their existence by proving, beyond a shadow of a doubt, that it was not Beauty but Duty that interested the early Anglo-Catholics.[4] Ritualistic observances are to be adopted because they are commanded in the Rubrics. As yet there is only occasional mention of the fact that a more ceremonious service might draw more souls to the Church. Seduction of the sense by splendour is left to Rome.[5] Why should the English Church submit to a Puritan bareness that violates its own laws? The argument at this stage seldom goes farther. By far the greatest emphasis is placed on Dogma, and consequently the typical scene is a disputation. The novels are concerned with a serious business—they must prove that certain practices and beliefs are according to the literal words of the Bible itself, or equally binding Church traditions. For one who loves theological disputation (a taste more widespread than it is the fashion to admit) *Bernard Leslie* or *Margaret Percival*[6] are gold mines. But, obviously, fiction is not the better *as fiction* for resembling a dissertation. And the early novels are legalistic in another way—like Newman—like the Oxford Movement itself—in their respect for political geography. The question is not what is Truth, to be apprehended by the human

---

[4] See also Sewell, Elizabeth, *Margaret Percival* (1847), I, xxvi, 197.
[5] Paley, *The Church Restorers*, XI, 128.
[6] See below, Ch. XI.

spirit, but what is Truth in Our Church, coextensive with the
political boundaries of Great Britain. Here is another English
resemblance to the ancient Hebrew, and this does not come
from the Puritans. The Tractarians did not argue that barbarians outside Holy England should become Anglo-Catholic.

Soon after 1850, a great change in method and spirit was to
come over the novel.[7] But a certain development seems to have
taken place by the end of the 'forties as to the nature of the
tales reflecting the Oxford Movement, whatever the point of
view adopted. The early novels of Gresley, Paget, Tayler,
Long, and Fullerton, usually present only the writer's views—
the interlocutor is likely to agree with the spokesman, or merely
ask questions. But in *Loss and Gain, Margaret Percival,*[8] *Trevor, Alfred Lennox, Allerton and Dreux, Earlswood,* we often
have debates rather than one-sided discussions, and the opponents are given a chance to state their views. There may even
be sympathetic, though pitying, portrayal of the enemy. This
expansion is a preliminary to the growth of tolerance in the
'fifties. Still as hostile as ever to erroneous opinion, the combat-
ants were beginning to admit that Satan was clever enough to
win some who were neither knaves nor fools. The novels on
the Oxford Movement may be said to have passed in their first
ten years from the stage of illustrated sermon to the *Euphues*
stage of scholastic debate set in the frame of a very thin love
story.

Accompanying this change of tone had gone on continuous
experiment with the story interest. The narrative portions were
still, for the most part, definitely separate, forming a frame-
work built around the ideas. That is to say, one could ignore
the fiction without vitiating the exposition (though some illus-
trations might be lost), or one could remove the exposition

[7] See below, Part II, especially Chapter X.
[8] See below, Ch. XI.

entirely without making the plot unintelligible. But many attempts had been made to fuse these two elements, and the attempts were more frequent and more successful towards the end
of the period.[9] In those rare cases where the story seems to
be of more importance than the propaganda, it is usually melodrama. This is true of *Ellen Middleton,* and *Hawkstone,* and
of the crime stuff in *The Warden of Berkingholt.*

The real value of these religious tales, however, does not lie
in their compromises with cheap devices of literary excitement,—and, indeed, the best novels mentioned so far have not
sacrificed too much to plot,—but in their groping towards a
more serious fiction of ideas and manners, where intellectual
experience should take the place of the physical or erotic. In
speaking of Hawkstone, the hero in Armitage's *Ernest Singleton* says, "I think we ought to like to see 'novels' becoming
more serious and manly in tone, and not merely representing
the follies and foibles of fashionable life" or crime or unfortunate love.[10] The fiction we have discussed in this Part is
the early forerunner of the novels of Eliot, the "Philosophic
Romance," and the novel of ideas. And, it is not merely as
"predecessors," or even as historical documents, that these
books have their place. Newman and Disraeli need no defense.
The minor writers, while they are not worth the time of the
average busy man today, deserve their share of respect. Paget,
Gresley, and Heygate were able to think like men; that is,
their minds moved in the realm of social ideas. Their work
had an ethical backbone. Though their sphere was small and
conclusions questionable, they wrote not to titilate milady's
fancy in her idleness, but to advocate principles upon which men
should act.

[9] E.g., *Tancred, Loss and Gain, Trevor* (cf. Kingsley's early novels, below, Ch. IX).
[10] III, vi.

PART II. IN MID-VICTORIAN ENGLAND

CHAPTER VIII

NEW HOSTILITY

E VANGELICAL opposition to the Anglo-Catholic Movement continues to the present day, but by the middle of
the century it could be seen that this hostility had failed
to prevent the new school from winning a firm place in the
English Church and a share of the loaves and fishes. Fiction
dealing with the Oxford Movement ceased to be primarily a
debate between ecclesiastical extremists. A shift in the field
of battle was effected by a series of developments that reached
a peak in 1850. The gradual advance of the Movement would,
in time, have brought it before the general public. But sensational events hastened the process. The growing confidence
and daring of the Anglo-Catholics had carried them nearer
Rome—indeed, many of them "toppled over." The greatest
Tractarian leader, Newman, seceded to Rome in 1845. Before
that could be forgotten, England's Protestant suspicion and
anger were aroused by a move from an entirely different
quarter. This was the "Papal Aggression" of 1850, reëstablish-
ing a Roman Catholic hierarchy in England. Papal Vicars-
Apostolic were replaced by Bishops bearing territorial titles.
The Pope declared that "the time has come in which that form
of ecclesiastical government may be restored in England which
freely prevails in other countries."[1] Cardinal Wiseman, now

[1] Quoted in Cornish, *The English Church in the Nineteenth Century,* I,
342.

Archbishop of Westminster, spoke of the restoration of Catholic England to its orbit in the ecclesiastical firmament. The panic that ensued in England was one of the things which led Disraeli to abandon Tractarianism.[2] He describes the excitement thus:

> The country at first was more stupified than alarmed. It was conscious that something extraordinary had happened, and some great action taken by an ecclesiastical power, which from tradition it was ever inclined to view with suspicion and some fear. [Then the prime minister published a manifesto denouncing the aggression of the Pope.] A confused public wanted to be led and now they were led. They sprang to their feet like an armed man. The corporation of London, the universities of Oxford and Cambridge had audiences with the Queen; the counties met, the municipalities memorialized; before the first of January there had been held nearly seven thousand public meetings, asserting the supremacy of the Queen and calling on Her Majesty's Government to vindicate it by stringent measures.[3]

It might seem that the restoration of the "true" Catholic hierarchy in England would be considered an insult to Tractarian claims, rather than as part of the same movement, but the public took the opposite attitude and trembled at the whole Catholic Revival. Lord John Russell, the prime minister, in his denunciation of the "Papal Aggression," also attacked the Puseyite clergymen as "unworthy sons of the Church of England herself,"[4] who, by honour paid to saints, the use of the cross, and other Catholic practices and doctrines, led their flocks to the very verge of the precipice.[5] One novel in 1854 speaks of "Times like these . . . when the agents of the Romish

---

[2] Monypenny and Buckle, *op. cit.*, III, 271.
[3] *Endymion*, III, xxxi, 308-310.
[4] Quoted in Cornish, *op. cit.*, I, 347.
[5] Thureau-Dangin, *op. cit.*, II, 205.

antichrist are so busy drawing souls from the truth," especially
through the Tractarian party, "traitors within."[6] It became
necessary for the Anglo-Catholics, in self-defense, to emphasize the distinction between Anglican and Roman. Whereas
the first part of Gresley's *Bernard Leslie* (1842) had been
concerned almost entirely with advocating Catholic worship in
the place of Evangelical, his *Bernard Leslie. Second Part,* of
1859, is largely devoted to marking the boundaries that separate the Anglo-Catholic from Rome.

Not long after Newman's secession, Elizabeth F. S. Harris
published two tales advising Anglicans to remain in the English Church. In *From Oxford to Rome: and How it Fared with
Some who Lately Made the Journey* (1847), Eustace A. is
a gentleman engaged to an heiress. But his last months at the
university fill him with interests "in which the syren voice of
lady's love had no place,"[7] and he becomes an advocate of
celibacy. He receives ordination, and goes to work in a parish
where "division and disunion" "were marking the course of
the revival of the Church's ancient Holy Customs among a
people half puritanised by spirtual indolence, and half be-
witched from all true faith and discipline by the growing
spirit of rationalism of the age."[8] Then, under detached heads,
the chief features of his parochial life are presented. Eustace
advances in his doubt of Anglicanism, and is advised by a
venerated friend at Oxford to "put aside argumentative
thought, and travel and *feel.*"[9] We are warned of the dangers
of passively associating ourselves with the Roman Church
when in foreign countries, in a passage strangely anticipatory
of Eliot's philosophy:

[6] B—.M.E.S., *Experience,* I, 6, 7.
[7] II.
[8] III, 27-28.
[9] IV, 110.

Providence invests every act with inevitable conditions, which the unwise seek to escape, which one and another boasts that he does not know—boasts that they do not touch him; but the boast is on his lips, the conditions are in his soul. When, by our own will—our own will, however it may be veiled with many words ... we quit our own and introduce ourselves into another's home, and because the pictures are finer than ours, and the perfumes richer, and the servitors obsequious, we pray to be suffered to remain and make it our abode, it is but the condition of our act, if by-and-by we find ourselves sitting sorrowfully alone, singing with sad hearts—

No home have we here in these halls of pride.[10]

Among the Italians, however, was found happily "no free discussion at every *table d'hôte* of the rights and *utility* of their spiritual fathers; no Universities, no Institute, giving a colour of law to insurrection and treason; no voices of base Novels and viler Journals were abroad among the people instilling fury and fratricide, and all things unholy. Faith, the faith of unsophisticated times, lingers yet in Italy."[11] Eustace and his sister, Augusta, join Rome. Eustace becomes a novice in an Italian monastery. He grows dissatisfied, and sees that having been placed by Providence in one state, and having deliberately chosen for himself another, "a repetition of such free choice and dedication is morally impossible."[12] The disappointment of one who has gone from the Anglican to the Roman Church is analyzed in long direct argument devoid of narrative.[13] There is also a sub-plot, if it may be so called, in which a woman's husband deserts her because of new celibate convictions.

The same author's *Rest in the Church* (1848) opens typi-

[10] IV, 111-112.
[11] IV, 115.
[12] VI, 165.
[13] VI, "The Dream Dispelled."

cally: "cities were lulling to an early rest."[14] The curate, Norman, realizes, in spite of his love for the beauty of the Church,
that romance is not religion. But he is discharged from his
place for Tractarian innovations.[15] There are many long arguments, especially for attention to the poor—"society has its
boundary lines of doing good—subscription, and so on—within them we may work, but not beyond—it is improper!" Yet
Christ was the "FRIEND of publicans and sinners."[16] In Norman's place, no new curate is appointed. The result in the
neglected village is first immorality, then the invasion of dissent. Finally Norman returns. He still has trials to face. For example, in his refusal to bury a child of dissenters in the same
part of the churchyard as the baptized, he needs great strength
to resist the pleas of the broken-hearted mother. But he is
now undisturbed in observance of the rubrics. Matins and Even-
song are said, every festival and vigil kept, and the priest faces
east in prayer.[17] Then, all of a sudden, with no development,
Norman joins Rome, because of her perfect ideal, mighty
saints, and "imperial claims."[18] In the conclusion, "we close
our little book with none the less earnest an aspiration that
the great Catholic principle it is designed to suggest may become, through its means, the ground to some one silent reader
of the blessedness which, by that principle's neglect, the heart
of the writer has missed and lost for ever as to this world. Still,
while thus, probably fortunately, refrained, there are those
things in regard to which it seems a duty of honesty to express again . . . first—The venture of dissent from the dogma
that THE CATHOLIC CHURCH has no branches . . . but

[14] I, 81.
[15] II.
[16] IV, 166.
[17] VII.
[18] VIII.

is singly and alone *The Roman Church.* . . ."[19] The moral is, rest in the Church in which God has placed you. The declared purpose of the book is to offer "a call to that Duty which is the first commandment of The Church . . . Obedience."[20]

Secessions, and later the "Aggression," seem to have awakened the secular portion of England to the fact that a Catholic revival was going on within her own Church. Hostility began to spring up in new places. Before this period, only novelists specifically interested in religion paid much attention to the Movement—but now great representative novelists introduced into their writing attacks on the Puseyites or on Catholicism in general. Liberals began to open fire on the Movement, which had begun, it will be recalled, as a reaction against Liberalism.

The Nemesis of Faith (1849), by James Anthony Froude, is semi-autobiographical, and in form like his *The Spirit's Trials*[21] (1847), wholly of the unfledged fiction of the controversial 'forties. The hero, Markham Sutherland, had early come under Catholicizing influences. Transubstantiation, celibacy of the clergy, and fasting were talked of favorably at his home.[22] But it was the influence of the gifted man that swayed him, for "while in fact we were only Newmanites, we fancied we were becoming Catholics."[23] In spite of doubts, Sutherland took orders. Then he resigned his living, went to Italy, fell in love with a married woman, and was saved from suicide by the accidental appearance of an old friend, now a priest. Then, feeling his guilt, he underwent penance and received conditional baptism. "But Markham's new faith fabric

[19] Conclusion, 341.
[20] Preface, p. vii.
[21] In *Shadows of the Clouds.*
[22] 122.
[23] 135, 126.

had been reared upon the clouds of sudden violent feeling"
and was sapped by doubt.[24] His life was a waste. The book
is strongly anti-Catholic: with such statements as that "the
Catholic church since the Reformation has produced no great
man of science, no statesman, no philosopher, no poet."[25] Much
of *The Nemesis of Faith* consists in letters or memoirs by the
hero. It is partly autobiographical narrative, but chiefly discussion of doctrines and ideas, with the plausible arguments all
on one side. The awkwardness of the structure may be illustrated by the fact that the letters dealing with Sutherland's
ordination precede the sketch of his boyhood. This combination of the theological essay with love-story furnishes a splendid example of the technique of the 'forties. The love introduced into this story is, of course, somewhat more illicit than
that admitted in non-liberal novels. With *The Nemesis of
Faith,* our War of the Novelists became dramatic. At the time,
Froude was a fellow at Exeter College, Oxford, and William
Sewell (author of *Hawkstone,* and brother of Elizabeth Sewell), was a tutor. In his class in the College, Sewell denounced
the volume, and then, before his audience, tore to pieces a copy
(not his own) and threw it in the fire. On the same day,
Froude resigned his fellowship.

Another early novelist of the liberal camp was Mary Matilda
Howard, who dedicated one novel to the memory of Thomas
Arnold.[26] She was not a sceptic, but of the Broad Church
school, which became prominent in the middle of the century.
In *Brampton Rectory: or, The Lesson of Life* (1849) Mr.
Oswald is Low-Liberal, but he intends to remove the pews from
his church, scrape off the whitewash, have daily service, eve-

[24] 226.
[25] 145.
[26] *Brampton Rectory.*

ning prayers, and more frequent communion.[27] Yet he says that it is unscriptural to exalt common prayer,[28] and that the Holy Catholic Church included all who believe in Christ and profess his Name.[29] The writer, as a Liberal, opposes not only the Anglo-Catholics, but also, in *Helen Tyrell* (1854)[30], the Evangelicals. Eliza Lynn, later Mrs. Linton, who was to write some fiction about Anglo-Catholics in the next period, already in *Realities* (1851) gives a hostile sketch of a High Churchman, and says that many young clergymen now combine the worst parts of Catholicism, emphasizing rites and discipline, with the worst parts of a Calvinistic belief in the election of a few and the damnation of the majority.[31]

Though in *Pendennis* (1848-50), such a man as Newman is spoken of with respect as passing over, "truth-impelled, to the enemy,"[32] and though Thackeray in *The Newcomes* (1853-55) shows sympathy (not belief) for Roman Catholicism, the latter novel presents a scathing picture of an Anglo-Catholic clergyman who is a humbug. Charles Honeyman is lazy, effeminate, luxurious, worldly, and popular among women. He is a liar, and cheats the poor. His church is made to pay by being managed as a show. There goes to the making of this picture a good measure of the animosity against the Oxford Movement that was exhibited by the Protestants at the time of the Papal Aggression. It is an Anglo-Catholic esthete who is here held up to scorn—an interesting attack, when we recall that the esthetic phase of the Movement did not reach its greatest importance until the next decade. On the other hand, Thackeray

[27] XII.
[28] V.
[29] XXIX.
[30] *The Youth and Womanhood of Helen Tyrell.*
[31] III, ii, 25.
[32] II, lxi, 251.

in the same novel satirizes, of course, his usual victims, the
Evangelicals and the worldly. Yet there is no trace of faith
in scientific materialism. The attitude of the author is rather
anticlerical but orthodox.

One of the most amusing of those novels of the 'fifties that
attack the Oxford Movement without being either Roman
Catholic or Low Church, is William John Conybeare's *Perversion; or the Causes and Consequences of Infidelity. A Tale
for the Times* (1856). Indeed, this novel also assaults posi-
tivism, Mormonism, scepticism, pantheism, atheism, and dilet-
tantism. It has considerable humor—not a quality to be expected in a Mid-Victorian novel setting out deliberately to study
the various snares that may lead a man away from Christianity.
And more wonderful still, it has a masculine vigor and realism.
Conybeare does not hesitate to range widely in the realm of
ideas, sketch the career of the mistress of "Lord Wrybbalde,"
lay a scene in a Mormon household, and include bigamy in the
plot. The chief Causes of Infidelity are the religious excesses
of the clergy, and the temptations to free thought at Oxford.
The hero, Charles, was so disgusted with the "Ultra-Protes-
tants" that he returned to Oxford ready to listen to the opposite school, at that time dominant. His imagination was captivated "by the charms of architecture and music, which
adorned the high-church system; and still more by its
'dim religious light,' its air of poetic mysticism and reverential reserve. . . ." He became a pupil of a tutor in
Aristotle's ethics, who made use of Aristotle chiefly
to construct arguments from his ethics in favor of Tractarianism. This tutor, Lapwing, "was addicted to the extemporaneous
formation of the most singularly sentimental and schoolgirl-
ish attachments. The objects of this weakness, however, were
always of his own sex . . . eternal love would be almost too tame

an expression for the endearments which he lavished upon"
favorite pupils "in succession. . . . He celebrated the praises of
their beauty in English sonnets and Latin lyrics." Charles became his idol, and under his influence bought a handsome ros-
ary of ebony and silver, practiced Gregorian chants, and made
a speech in praise of Laud. He was also attracted by a professor's daughter with High Church charms.

> Indeed it may be remarked in passing, that this faith is pecu-
> liarly suited to young ladies; for it encourages and utilises their ac-
> complishments, sets them upon embroidering altar cloths, illu-
> minating prayer-books, elaborating surplices, practising church
> music, carving credence tables, and a hundred other innocent diver-
> sions, which it invests with the prestige of religious duty. And be-
> sides this, it imposes no cruel prohibition (like the rival creed)
> upon their favorite amusements; but commends the concert, smiles
> upon the ball, and does not even anathematise the theatre. All these
> accomplishments . . . were displayed for the captivation of Charles
> Bampton, and not without success. [But his ecclesiastical ardour
> was chilled when he was "twice jilted . . . first by his tutor, and
> again by his mistress."][33]

Later, the author gives us a very amusing satirical portrait
of a club of free-thinkers.[34] They argue that indulgence of
physical impulses is innocent, and that only the gloomy code
of Christianity condemns them. So the hero's morals, as well
as his religion, are undermined. In the end, his sister, who
has forsaken her faith, commits suicide; Charles repents of
his sins and becomes a Christian. In technique, this novel shows
the new importance of story, realism, and humor. It even fore-
shadows the sex-sensationalism of the next period. Although
the structure is still rather primitive—in the main story episodes are interspersed wherein certain types of opinion are

[33] X, 177-184.
[34] XII.

ridiculed,—the episodes themselves are narrative and dramatic, not argumentative exchange of theory. Instead of the earlier method of propaganda by dogmatic dialogue, we are given examples of persons who hold certain opinions, and evil results are allowed to appear—with the implication that they are the natural consequence of the opinions. The plot does not yet grow out of character and setting, but it does grow out of the religious views of the participants. The advance of this novel towards intrinsic fictional interest and sound form is all the more significant because in substance it is an obscure novel, shallow, and frankly polemic.

George Borrow, in the "Preface to the First Edition" of *Lavengro: The Scholar—The Gypsy—The Priest* (1851), said that among the things attempted in this book was "the exposure of humbug . . . of which the most perfidious, the most debasing, and the most cruel, is the humbug of the Priest."[35] He attacks the Roman Church and the "favourers of priestcraft who lurked within the walls of the Church of England," for "in every country, however enlightened, there are always minds inclined to grovelling superstition—minds fond of eating dust, and swallowing clay—minds never at rest, save when prostrate before some fellow in a surplice."[36] He seems to think that the Papal Aggression has awakened England to the wickedness of Rome. He ascribes the Catholic Revival to the influence of Scott's novels, especially among the middle classes, whose "chief characteristic" one of the characters tells us "is a rage for grandeur and gentility. . . . All their conversation now is about gallant knights, princesses, and cavaliers, with which his pages are stuffed—all of whom were Papists, or very High Church, which is nearly the same thing; and they are

[35] 2.
[36] 3.

beginning to think that the religion of such nice sweet-scented
gentry must be something very superfine. Why, I know at Birmingham the daughter of an ironmonger, who screeches to
the piano the Lady of the Lake's hymn to the Virgin Mary,
always weeps when Mary Queen of Scots is mentioned, and
fasts on the anniversary of the death of that very wise martyr,
Charles the First."[37]

In the same author's *The Romany Rye* (1857), more is
said about the influence of Scott, on the Oxford Movement in
particular.[38] "So, owing to his rage for gentility, Scott must
needs become the apologist of the Stuarts and their party;
but God made this man pay dearly for taking the part of the
wicked against the good . . . God, who knows perfectly well
how and where to strike," deprived "the apologist of that
wretched crew of all that rendered life pleasant in his eyes,
the lack of which paralyzed him in body and mind, rendered
him pitiable to others, loathsome to himself. . . . He was not a
Papist himself, . . . for he had read enough of the Bible to
know that no one can be saved through Popery, yet had he
a sneaking affection for it, and would at times in an underhand
manner, give it a good word both in writing and discourse,
because it was a gaudy kind of worship, and ignorance and vas-
salage prevailed so long as it flourished."[39]

Charlotte Brontë is one of the most Protestant novelists
who has ever appeared, but not in a doctrinal sense—it is that
her very art, her interpretations of facts, her mood, reveal
a Protestant culture. Not that this was unconscious. She was
explicitly hostile to Catholicism, whether Anglican or Roman.
And much of what she attacked in Romanism was also found

[37] XCIV, 493-494 ("the man in black" speaking).
[38] Appendix: all of chapters VI, VII.
[39] Appendix VII, 354-355.

in Puseyism, as England in the center of the century was ex-
citedly learning. In her first novel, *The Professor*,[40] for example, occurs an attack on what the greatest Tractarian novelists were to praise so highly: the "tame, trained subjection" of
manner in a girl prepared to give up "her independence of
thought and action into the hands of some despotic confessor.
She permitted herself no original opinion."[41] In the opening
chapter of *Shirley* (1849), the author says that in 1811-12 "The
present successors of the apostles, disciples of Dr. Pusey and
tools of the Propaganda, were at that time being hatched under
cradle-blankets, or undergoing regeneration by nursery-bap-
tism in wash-hand-basins. You could not have guessed by looking at any one of them that the Italian-ironed double frills of
its net-cap surrounded the brows of a pre-ordained, especially
sanctified successor of St. Paul, St. Peter, or St. John. . . ."

Villette (1853) is a mature study of a Protestant soul in a
Catholic environment. Indeed, one feels that Charlotte Brontë
herself does not know quite how much Lucy Snowe is the
product of Protestantism, and her Belgian environment of
Catholicism. Nevertheless, the writer and her heroine are very
conscious of the conflict of religions. Lucy is somewhat afraid
of being seduced into Romanism if she permits herself too much
contact with a priest. And usually what she objects to belongs
to Catholicism as such, rather than merely to Rome. For example, she attacks saints' lives,[42] and she states her faith thus to
M. Paul, her Catholic lover:

> I told him how we kept fewer forms between us and God; retain-
> ing, indeed, no more than, perhaps, the nature of mankind in the
> mass rendered necessary for due observance. I told him I could

[40] Posthumously published in 1857.
[41] XII, 88.
[42] XIII, 102-103.

not look on flowers and tinsel, on wax-lights and embroidery, at
such times and under such circumstances as should be devoted to
lifting the secret vision to Him whose home is Infinity, and His
being—Eternity. That when I thought of sin and sorrow, of earthly corruption, mortal depravity, weighty temporal woe—I could
not care for chanting priests or mumming officials; that when the
pain of existence and the terrors of dissolution pressed before me—
when the mighty hope and measureless doubt of the future arose
in view—*then,* even the scientific strain, or the prayer in a language learned and dead, harassed with hindrance a heart which
only longed to cry—
  "God be merciful to me, a sinner!"[43]

The psychology, the esthetics, the very soul of the Puritan
have seldom been set forth with more profundity or more dark
and powerful eloquence. And yet the authority appealed to is
not the Bible, but the reader's experience or feeling. And Charlotte Brontë is, of course, a very secular novelist, not at all
one of the Evangelicals whose warfare we spoke of in an
earlier chapter. She, like Eliot, is a link between Protestantism
and its child, Naturalism, and, at least to that extent, she stands
with the Liberals.

Though minor controversial fiction continued to be written,
it no longer held the chief place among novels touching upon
the Oxford Movement. The casual references of a Thackeray
or the underlying feeling of a Brontë are of much more literary
interest. And, except in fiction produced by the Evangelicals
themselves, the Evangelical is no longer the chief opponent of
the Anglo-Catholic. New lines of battle are being drawn up,
and it is possible to perceive a corresponding change in narrative method. Concerned now not with proving literal accord
with the Bible, or the possession of supernatural sanctions, the
novels of the 'fifties are truer novels—studies of human life—

[43] XXXVI, 384.

not dogmatic arguments conducted by undramatic dialogue and supported by references. Perhaps the appearance on the field of the Liberals led the Protestants and Anglo-Catholics alike to carry the battle to the Liberals' own ground, and think more of human instinct and general welfare, less of quotable authority; more of the lay world, less of the ecclesiastical. We are not now so likely to be told of a character (for example) that he united all the worst elements in the Evangelical system, though he lived a blameless life.[44]

[44] Paget, *The Warden of Berkingholt,* II, 42-43 ("The services in the Prayer-book which he happened to dislike, he mutilated; parts, as the Athanasian Creed, he never read at all.")

CHAPTER IX

CHARLES KINGSLEY: LIBERAL ANTAGONIST

THE most important novels actually called forth, at least in part, by the Oxford Movement, were those of Charles Kingsley. Among the hundreds of volumes—fiction, verse, theology, scholarship,—produced by the Movement, *pro* and *con*, probably *Hypatia* is the one book which is now considered indispensable in the education of a complete gentleman. As one of the leading writers of the novel of purpose, and as the great antagonist of the Movement, whose attacks finally gave Newman an opening for the *Apologia*, Kingsley, his portrayal of the Tractarians, and his criticism of their views, deserve a central position in our study.

His hostility was based upon opposition in the one most fundamental question of all ethical, social, or religious thinking: Whereas Newman and the Anglo-Catholics agreed with the Calvinists in believing that human nature is sinful, unless regenerated by the Grace of God, Kingsley belonged to the third "Christian" religion, which has faith in the goodness of the Natural. The Neo-Humanists would be correct in saying that Kingsley is of the school of Rousseau. Indeed, the whole Reactionary Revolution—the Oxford Movement—New-Toryism—Neo-Catholicism—had for its avowed object of warfare just that extreme Rousseauistic faith in the goodness of the natural man and the consequent belief in democracy and moral liberty. Of the Goths, Kingsley was in his day a mighty champion, and preferred to look for true men and true worship outside the Empire of Rome. His trust in nature flows in many channels that are joined together in a common source. With reference to the external universe, it takes the form of a thorough faith in science; which means (translated into human terms), he believes that knowledge about the physical world, arrived at through experiment and speculation unfettered by *a priori* formulæ, will increase the sum of happiness. Claude Mellot, with the author's support, approves of Mechanics' Institutes.[1] Kingsley makes sanitation a subject for romantic enthusiasm, and even shows Unsanitary Conditions as a sort of brooding evil productive of tragedy.[2] In *Yeast,* Lancelot answers his cousin, a Tractarian curate, by saying that nature must be a revelation of God; "spiritual laws must be in perfect harmony with every fresh physical law which we discover . . . the spiritual cannot be intended to be perfected by ignoring or crushing the physical. . . . So give me the political economists, the sanitary reformer, the engineer; and take your saints and virgins, relics, and miracles."[3] In *Alton Locke,* the Dean speaks of "the inner ideas, the spirit of Nature, which is the will of God."[4]

Protestantism in Kingsley usually means reliance on natural instinct (as opposed to the acceptance of a celibate ideal), on the natural man's understanding of the Bible (as opposed to interpretation under guidance of the Church) and on the natural conclusions of human intellect (obedient to no previously accepted doctrine). The religion which had set up the individual three centuries before as the final judge of the mean-

---

[1] *Two Years Ago,* Introductory, 6. See explanation of Mechanics' Institutes below, p. 128.

[2] E.g., *Yeast,* XIII, 192-3; *Alton Locke,* II, xxxix; *Two Years Ago,* II, xvii ("Baalzebub's Banquet").

[3] V, 70-71.

[4] II, xxxviii, 247.

ing of the Bible had in it the seeds of Rationalism. Ultimately, the Protestant might be allowing the unrestrained reason not only to interpret but to criticize the Scriptures, as it had long ago criticized the Church. By no accident was Germany the home of Rationalism and Higher Criticism. But it is certainly old Protestant prejudice rather than reliance on human nature which speaks in *Westward Ho!* where we are told that, after the Spanish Armada was vanquished, "the everlasting war which is in heaven" between Light and Darkness was lulled for a while—a war which slowly ripens into a day of judgment once in many centuries and becomes then incarnate,

> no longer a mere spiritual fight, but one of flesh and blood, wherein simple men may choose their sides without mistake, and help God's cause not merely with prayer and pen, but with sharp shot and cold steel. A day of judgment has come, which has divided the light from the darkness, and the sheep from the goats. . . .

The devil's work collapses at the merest pin prick in these combats, and the children of Israel as of old see the Egyptians dead on the sea-shore.[5]

But novels have for their subject matter not only brooding forces, the concepts of science, and theology, but also human problems. And here it was that Kingsley shocked the orthodox. It may seem innocent enough to say, abstractly, that you trust in nature. But when a Victorian clergyman of the "Anglican branch of the Holy Catholic Church" says that natural passions are good, when he gives this doctrine flesh and blood in dramatic narrative that women and the young will read, once again a theological proposition has shown itself to have more than scholastic meaning. Kingsley believed that we are naturally monogamous, and that the highest life involves love of one man for one woman, sanctified by—one might say a love

[5] III, xii.

that itself sanctifies—the sacrament of matrimony. In Victorian England there were not many who advocated the now popular dogmas of polygamous or, rather, promiscuous privileges, and those who fulminated against the sinfulness of marriage were few. In that direction not much defence was necessary, although Kingsley did put into the mouth of Raphael Aben-Ezra an interpretation of the Song of Solomon as a praise of monogamy, wherein the great king forgets his threescore queens and fourscore concubines and virgins without number for the pure love of one.[6] But the arch-enemy threatening to obliterate wedded love for the Victorian clergyman was not Radicalism but the doctrine of the superiority of celibacy. When the Oxford Tracts appeared, Kingsley fiercely denounced the ascetic views which he saw would be their result.[7] The hero of *Yeast* writes to his Tractarian cousin that God made his appetites a part of him, while "you and yours make piety a synonym for unmanliness,"[8] and later he tells his sweetheart that she has taught him "that which is most luscious is also the most pure."[9] In *Hypatia*, Raphael, a Jew, attacks the idea that a Deity would derive pleasure from the celibacy of a girl; and he reserves his faith for some God who "takes no delight in seeing his creatures stultify the primary laws of their being."[10] Raphael's mother speaks of herself as a nun, "fattening her own mad self-conceit upon the impious fancy that she was the spouse of the Nazarene . . ."[11] and says that the Christians and philosophers consider it brutal to be a man and not a monk or eunuch. "Ay, and the only man who keeps his manhood, the

[6] *Hypatia*, II, vi.
[7] *Charles Kingsley, His Letters and Memories of His Life,* I, 45.
[8] II, 26-28.
[9] VII, 97.
[10] II, ii.
[11] II, xv.

only man who is not ashamed to be what God has made him, is
your Jew."[12] Indeed, in *Yeast,* Claude Mellot argues that Protestant clergymen should have long beards, "testifying that the
essential idea of Protestantism is the dignity and divinity of
man as God made him."[13]

One of the fruits of reliance on instinct is a faith in the
"lower orders," since all men are gifted with instinct, and an
unusually noble conscience, according to ethical naturalists, is
as likely to appear among the poor as among those who have
received an expensive education. Kingsley goes so far as to
say that the Bible is the history of mankind's deliverance from
all tyranny, the Jews then the one free constitutional people
in a world of slaves, and the New Testament the good news
that freedom, brotherhood, and equality, once confined to
Greece and Judaea, were to become the right of all mankind.[14]
The hero of *Yeast,* a gentleman in the British sense, tells a discharged game-keeper, a Dissenter, Tregarva, "I will go [to
a wake] with Paul Tregarva, whom I honour and esteem as
one of God's own noblemen; who has taught me what a man
can be, and what I am not."[15] At which all advocates of deco-
rum and taste and order might well raise a protest. But Kingsley was only a Christian Socialist, not a revolutionist. Chartism, by insisting on its own program instead of submitting to
God's will, has, says Eleanor, in *Alton Locke,* "defiled itself
in the eyes of the wise, the good, the gentle."[16]

Kingsley relies on the individual conscience, and classes
Catholic spiritual direction with alcohol and opium as the three

[12] II, xi.
[13] III, 42.
[14] *Alton Locke,* II, xxx, 155-156.
[15] XI, 154.
[16] II, xl, 257-258.

best means of attaining mere peace of mind.[17] (Anticipating Soviet Russia.) His suspicion that Catholicism is not intellectually honest became famous because his accusations against Newman were answered in the *Apologia*. But, years before, in *Yeast*, the Tractarian curate (later a convert to Rome) had written that he could not sympathize with "that superstitious reverence for mere verbal truth which is so common among Protestants." If the Protestants believed the nature of man, *including his intellect*, corrupt, they would not be so careful to tell the truth. "The proper use of reasoning is to produce opinion." Lancelot's answer is typical of Kingsley's thought: All sound intellect is divine light, and Protestants "reverence facts as the work of God."[18]

Having sketched the ideas relative to the Oxford Movement presented in Kingsley's novels, we must speak of the novels individually before considering the author's literary method, closely related as it is to his philosophy. We have shown that, immediately after the Papal Aggression (1850), there were a number of attacks upon Catholicism. Kingsley, perhaps because he was a clergyman, and therefore closer to the Movement, had already begun his fictional opposition in *Yeast*, which ran in *Fraser's Magazine* from July to December, 1848. But this version gave less space to the attack upon the Tractarians than the revised edition of 1851, which added Chapters V, VIII, and XV, and the Epilogue. The novel in its final form is still as chaotic as most of the controversial tales of the 'forties, and its method, spirit, and interests are of the same school, though it is raised into the aristocratic circle of literature by the style, emotion, and original pictures of Eng-

---

[17] *Yeast*, XII, 165.
[18] X, 136-137.

lish life. We have a Dissenter of noble character, and, in contrast, a High Church vicar and a High Church curate, both of whom trifle with the truth. Both are finally converted to Rome. We have a lady heroine romantically concerned with being religious, who intends to enter a sort of Anglican convent, but finds that her "womanhood" cannot withstand the "manly will" of her lover, that is, as he points out, God is leading her to him.[19] Kingsley begs the reader to remember that the author is in no way responsible for the speculations either of the hero or of his acquaintances,[20] but if a pamphleteer is advancing certain theories,—a pamphleteer who hides his sympathies as little as Kingsley,—it is usually fairly obvious when the arguments are supposed to be convincing and when they are supposed to be ridiculous. In spite of the author's attempt to shield himseld behind his *dramatis personæ*, *Yeast* made him enemies.[21]

It was difficult to find a publisher for the next novel, *Alton Locke* (1850). Refused by Messrs. Parker, who thought they had suffered in reputation for publishing *Yeast* (in *Fraser's Magazine*), it was accepted by Chapman and Hall upon Carlyle's recommendation.[22] Mrs. Locke, Alton's mother, was a thorough-going Calvinist.—Her form of Protestantism is almost as hostile to Liberalism as Catholicism itself, and Kingsley knows it.—She hated and feared Babylon (temptations of London) as she did Bishops, and believed in infant damnation, election, predestination, and the wickedness of Sunday amusements. And this in a generation when "the daily discoveries of science are revealing [God's] love in every microscopic animalcule which peoples the stagnant pool!"[23] Her re-

---

[19] X, 141.
[20] XIV, 199.
[21] *Charles Kingsley, His Letters (etc.).* I, 246, 282.
[22] *Ibid.,* I, 233.
[23] I, i, 115.

ligion was an "infernal superstition which taught her to fancy
. . . that God could hate His creature, not for its sins but for
the very nature which He had given it."[24] The hero is a Chartist. Some High Church figures appear as rather ineffectual.
The novel concludes with arguments for Christian Socialism.
Though the form is autobiographical, and Alton is more radical than Kingsley, again we feel that the author has not concealed his own voice.

Hypatia, (1853), has for a subtitle *New Foes with an Old
Face*. The new foes are those nineteenth-century currents that
might break up the family and the rule of the people in a nation: asceticism, scepticism, aristocracy, theocracy. The old
face is the Empire of the fifth century. In 1851 Kingsley writes
to Maurice that the notion of such a historical romance has
been breeding in his head for two years. "My idea . . . is to
set forth Christianity as the only really democratic creed."[25]
It opens with a young monk, Philammon, finding for the first
time that women are beautiful, and that he must have liberty.
In Alexandria, he plunges into the dying world of Paganism,
with all its refinement, art, and learning typified in the beautiful Hypatia, but a world also cruel, sensual, sceptical, and
weary. The historical imagination has seldom achieved anything so magnificent as this picture of society in decay, of a
civilization that has lost heart, and devoid of unity or hope, is
breaking down into cults and parties and hard ambition. Only
Petronius has surpassed Kingsley in giving us a picture of
Rome ageing horribly, and Petronius could not show the young
Teutons as the destined heirs of the treasure whose owner was
rotting away. Besides Classical decadents and splendid Bar-

[24] II, xix, 35.
[25] Letter to Maurice, Jan. 16, 1851. *Charles Kingsley, His Letters (etc.)*,
I, 264.

barians, Philammon also meets with Christian monks, represented as a fanatical mob, and the leaders of the Church, bick-
ering in petty jealously and fighting for place and power. He
finds the Church with its councils rent by intrigue a travesty
on Christianity. When the monks tear Hypatia to death, it
is a symbol of the worst in superstition destroying the best in
Classical culture. And this, according to Kingsley, was the
Church of the Fathers, whose doctrine nineteenth-century
Englishmen had been told to obey without question, though it
might condemn Greek philosophy, supplement the teachings of
Solomon and of Jesus beyond recognition, ignore the wisdom
that coming centuries of Christian thought were to develop,
disagree with the conclusions of science or scholarship, and
defy the democratic hopes of a progressive nation. The Anglo-
Catholics went back, not to the Bible, but to the Early Church
for ideas that would be valid for all time, and Kingsley's
picture of that Church was the most devastating shell that
had exploded among them since the seventeenth century. It was
high time for Newman's *Callista,* whose purpose was to express, "from a Catholic point of view, the feelings and mutual relations of Christians and heathens" in the third century.[26] And it was little wonder High Churchmen should not
want to give Kingsley an honorary degree, or that *Hypatia*
should be called an immoral book, "and one calculated to encourage young men in profligacy and false doctrine."[27] Nor
is it surprising that, in time, he should be appointed Professor of History at Cambridge, a center of Protestantism, Platonism, and Liberalism, since before Spenser.

Westward Ho! (1855) was written during the Crimean
War. In a letter to Maurice, October 19, 1854, Kingsley says

[26] Advertisement, vii.
[27] *Charles Kingsley, His Letters (etc.),* II, 179.

that it is dreadful not to be with the army, "But I can fight with my pen still (I don't mean in controversy—I am sick of that.) . . . but in writing books which will make others fight. This one is to be called 'Westward Ho!' "[28] Nevertheless, the novel is about the conflict between Protestant England and Catholic Spain, or, as Kingsley actually tells us in the novel, sheep *versus* goats.[29] The religious differences receive emphasis throughout. Indeed, the novel is well designated in the High Church *Christian Remembrancer* as "an outburst of burly triumphant Protestantism and nationality."[30]

Controversy has more visibly died down when we reach *Two Years Ago* (1857). The Catholic Revival is merely touched in passing, or rather *used* as any other element in English life might be. It is no longer a real key to the whole work. Such merely incidental treatment of the Oxford Movement is to be characteristic of many novels in the 'sixties and 'seventies. *Two Years Ago* illustrates, also, what is not necessarily the same thing, the new tolerance that grew all through the 'fifties. Frank Headley, a Puseyite curate, is a fine chap, though his labors among the people fail to win confidence at first because he is suspected of Popery. Frank "had nothing, save the outside, in common with those undesirable coxcombs, who have not been bred by the High Church movement, but have taken refuge in its cracks."[31] Later, Frank learns to forget that he is a priest and to meet people "upon the commonest human grounds."[32] The picture of the Oxford Movement in this novel, as compared with that in *Yeast* and *Alton Locke*, suggests that there has been a development towards alliance be-

[28] *Ibid.*, I, 433.
[29] III, xii.
[30] *Christian Remembrancer*, XXXIV, xcviii, Oct. 1857, p. 394.
[31] I, ii, 63-64.
[32] II, xvii, 86.

tween Anglo-Catholicism and humanitarism.[33] This is confirmed by other novels.[34]

Even in his *Water-Babies: A Fairy-Tale for a Land-Baby* (1863) there is an attack on monks.[35]

The key to the art, as well as to the thought, of Kingsley's novels is found in reliance on nature. The author's plots are not deterministic, like those of the later naturalists. We find little of the careful preparation of cause for consequence, little descriptive emphasis upon environment, little subjective analysis. Nor does he play upon sensational, criminal, and sexual excitement like the authors of a later day, less complacent in their philosophy. In Kingsley, "natural" must often be defined as that which is accepted by the average Englishman of the time. The plots of even *Yeast* and *Alton Locke* are built around love affairs. That is seldom true of the Anglo-Catholic novels of the same period. Granted that Kingsley is in accord with the method of the latter to the extent that the love affairs should often not culminate happily,[36] nevertheless, he remains at the end unresigned to such an outcome, or shows it to be the result of evil forces in society. In Newman's plots, the characters are led by the voice of God. In Disraeli, they often meet a Jew, who gives them advice. In Kingsley they lead themselves, trusting their own emotions.—The same three sources of guidance were recommended, respectively, in answer to the question, "What will save England?" (not asked for the first time in the twentieth century). Kingsley, confident that the English have their source of strength in themselves, writes historical novels in praise of the national past,[37] just as Disraeli

---

[33] E.g., I, ii, 64.
[34] See below, Chapter XIII.
[35] V, 208-209.
[36] E.g., in *Yeast, Alton Locke, Hypatia.*
[37] Add *Hereward the Wake* to those I have discussed.

carries his readers to Palestine, and Newman to Rome. Even in *Hypatia* the only healthy people in the Roman Empire are the Teutonic barbarians.

In motivation as in plot, sexual love is a mainspring much more important than in the Anglo-Catholic novels. Already a different dogma is leading to a different psychology. Moreover, Kingsley does at least foreshadow naturalistic determinism in showing one cause for sin and misery in a background of social conditions, for which, indeed, individuals are often responsible. Dialogue in Kingsley does not consist in logical steps intellectually developed, as in Newman, or the sparkle of programs wittily put, as in Disraeli, but in the expression of feeling or the proposal of hypotheses. His reliance on instinct is shown in the fact that the arguments do not seem to lead to definite dogmatic conclusions, but are left hanging. In constructing an outline of his philosophy, one must select somewhat insecurely from diverse statements, usually by heroes with whom the author does not entirely agree. Now there is never any doubt about what Newman means. But when it came to writing drama, or creating different characters, the man who sympathized with only one creed, was far surpassed by the one whose opinions were less definite.

There are few authors more British or more Victorian than Kingsley, with his reliance on instinct, his capacity for compromise, and his admiration for action.[38] He holds to the Athanasian Creed[39] and to Science. He defends a form of confession,[40] and yet is a pugnacious Protestant—and also a "socialist." His is that national genius which is able to pass from old to new without unduly disturbing the peace of mind or

[38] Cf., *Alton Locke*, II, xxx, 154-155. (That the strength of the clergy lies in action.)

[39] *Charles Kingsley, His Letters (etc.)*, II, 394.

[40] *Yeast*, X, 130.

of society, a genius particularly in evidence during the Victorian Age. Though Kingsley's pictures of Tractarians are so obviously prejudiced that it is hardly necessary to correct them, his comments help to reveal the core of his own vigorous mind, and the setting of the Oxford Movement within the framework of other mid-century ideas. He struck some of the most sounding blows ever dealt against the Puseyites, choosing to crush the heads of his foes with a frank Northern stroke, thereby making the battle noiser and bloodier, and earning the gratitude of all of us today. Especially of Anglo-Catholics. Someone has said that since we have lost Satan, no one has been much interested in God. Without Kingsley, the Oxford Movement would lack epic proportions. He was not only a warrior himself, but an excuse for belligerence in others. Without Kingsley, there might have been no *Apologia Pro Vita Sua*.

CHAPTER X

CHARLOTTE MARY YONGE, AND THE NOVEL OF DOMESTIC MANNERS

WE HAVE indicated that the end of the 'forties saw a diminution of the sectarian virulence in this War of the Novels,[1] but also an extension of the area of conflict. Our survey of the hostility that sprang up against the Movement in new places has carried us well into the 'fifties. In Kingsley we have analyzed the basis of his typical liberal opposition, and in spite of this author's unusual amount of pugnacity we have found in his novels a gradual development away from the purpose-novel. In this evolution, Kingsley was representative of England at large. When propaganda was carried on now, it was less by means of the frankly controversial novel, more by giving proper coloring to a novel of manners. We do not actually get away from prejudiced portrayal of the Anglo-Catholics until we reach Trollope.

A contemporary observer, writing of Tractarian fiction, remarks (and this would apply equally well to the novels of the opposition): "By degrees, as these [Catholic] doctrines became more and more clearly understood and acted on, the religious tale dropped its expository conversations and its preachments, and allowed the thread of the story to go on unbroken, trusting to the general tone of the whole to impress the reader with the great practical truths which hang upon, and accompany the belief of doctrinal truth; faith is illustrated

[1] Ch. VII.

more by the life of the character described than by mere
theological terms by which it may be expressed."[2] In the fiction
dealing with the Oxford Movement, the contrast is marked,
between the 'forties dominated by the controversial novel and
the 'fifties dominated by the novel of manners. The earlier tales
had been, almost without exception, bellicose in purpose, tone,
and even, with their long arguments, in the very nature of the
scenes portrayed. The slight difference (sketched in Part I)
between the fiction-framed, one-sided exposition and the somewhat later fusion, or, rather, unfused addition, of a love story
and a two-sided debate, though this development was in the
direction of the legitimate novel, was itself less striking than
the contrast between the romanced-debate and the form of fiction which was next brought to bear upon the Oxford Movement.

While there were much better artists writing novels of manners at this time,[3] for our purposes the best way to demonstrate
the characteristics of the form will be to analyze the method of
Charlotte Mary Yonge. For, whereas in controversial fiction
all sides have an equal opportunity, in novels portraying the
daily life of Anglo-Catholics, a Tractarian author naturally has
the advantage. And Miss Yonge was the greatest of all purely
Anglo-Catholic novelists in the Victorian Age.[4] Not only for
us, but in any final estimate of her work, Miss Yonge's claim
to a position in literature depends on her success with the

[2] "The Moral Character of Story Books," *Christian Remembrancer,* XL,
cix, July, 1860, p. 61.
[3] E.g. Mrs. Gaskell's *Ruth* (and her *Cranford*) was published in the
same year as Miss Yonge's masterpiece, *The Heir of Redclyffe,* 1853.
[4] Newman, by the time he wrote his novels, was a Romanist. Shorthouse
retained a trace of his liberal origins; Disraeli was only parallel; Trollope
and Thackery secular; Kingsley, Brontë, and Reade definitely in opposition.

Tractarian novel during its phase as novel of contemporary manners. A character in Oliphant's *Phoebe Junior* (1876) says that "one reads Scott for Scotland (and a few other things), and one reads Miss Yonge for the church. Mr. Trollope is good for that, too, but not so good. All that I know of clergymen's families I have got from her."[5] Another writer says: "There can be no doubt that the writings of Charlotte Yonge have inspired more than two generations of readers with the enthusiastic belief in the truth and office of the Church of England, and in its historic continuity with the Church of Augustine and Anselm."[6] For many years John Keble himself read in manuscript everything written by Miss Yonge.[7]

Much of her writing was "for the young," and, indeed, there is a touch of the juvenile about all of her novels. We shall try not to include purely juvenile fiction, but it is impossible to draw the line with absolute precision. One novel is designated in its preface as neither a tale for the young nor a novel for their elders, but a mixture of both.[8] Indeed, some of the more conservative still considered novels food largely for women and babes, though by the time Miss Yonge became known as a novelist, *Vanity Fair* had been in print for five years. Miss Yonge's plots are usually complicated, and since it is not the plot but the life that is of value in these novels, it would be an irrelevance for us to give synopses.

If *Hypatia* was the greatest work produced by the enemies of the Oxford Movement, *The Heir of Redclyffe,* published in the same year, 1853, was the most famous of all the novels written by Tractarians. The hero, Sir Guy Morville, though

[5] II, ix, 175.
[6] Cavendish in Romanes, *Charlotte Mary Yonge,* 200; Cf. Escott, *Anthony Trollope,* 223.
[7] Romanes, *Charlotte Mary Yonge,* 32.
[8] *The Daisy Chain* (1856), p. iii.

badly in need of the colloquial advice, "Be your age"—it is hard to realize that this boy was supposed to represent a young man—is, nevertheless, a charming character. He is what so many heroes of Anglo-Catholic fiction were meant to be, a saint and a gentleman. (How that combination would have disgusted the old High and Dry aristocrats!) He dies from a disease contracted in nursing his fever-stricken enemy, Philip. The hero is thus removed while the book still has a fifth of the way to go, a rather violent way to avoid a happy culmination of love, even for a Tractarian novel.[9] Sir Guy is not only an enthusiast, but a gentleman, in the narrower social sense. Indeed, Miss Yonge preaches the duty of a certain amount of worldliness. When Guy is rebellious enough to think social life dangerously pleasant, he is told that he cannot lay aside his position in society merely because it is full of trial—that would be to fail in trust in Him who fixed his station.[10]

When Miss Yonge's brother got his commission in the army, she "compared it to a young squire obtaining knighthood, and felt it to be a sort of revival of the romance of an older day."[11] She was at that time almost thirty years of age. With so real a tendency to gild the lily, it is not surprising that she produced, in *The Heir of Redclyffe,* the best example of Victorian life Medievalized. Like so many Anglo-Catholic novelists, admiring the age that Scott had glorified, she made the nineteenth century look as much as possible like the earlier epoch.[12] Religious, social, esthetic traces of the Middle Ages which still lingered in Victorian England, or had been revived, she printed in rubrics, and lo! the objectionable world of Democracy, In-

[9] See above, Ch. VII.
[10] IV, 50.
[11] Coleridge, *Charlotte Mary Yonge,* 168.
[12] Cf. William Sewell, Disraeli, Shorthouse.

dustry, and Science vanished! Sir Guy is of high birth, he is pure, chivalric, Catholic. He is on the quest of religious excellence, yet, next to the Church, his lady love has all his heart. He is the monarch, the young prince, of Redclyffe, surrounded by feudal loyalty. He might almost be a petty ruler of an independent principality, rather than a citizen of a united Parliamentary nation. The novel fuses this Feudal with an Esthetic Medievalism in its self-conscious innocence, its careful attention to details, its convention-charged "simplicity." Over the Pre-Raphaelites the novel "exercised an extraordinary fascination." While the group was still at Oxford, Sir Guy "was adopted by them as a pattern for actual life: and more strongly perhaps by Morris than by the rest, from his own greater wealth and more aristocratic temper."[13]

But the Pre-Raphaelites were not the only ones among whom *The Heir of Redclyffe* had a great success. Ethel Romanes says that "many of us are fain to confess to having read it at least a score of times."[14] Miss Yonge's brother in the army found that nearly all the young men in his regiment had a copy of the book. "Scholarly gentlemen wept over Guy's death, and what is far more important, trying to be very good was made interesting and romantic to thousands of good girls. The interesting note in a hero was no longer wickedness but goodness." Miss F. M. Peard said that enthusiasm for Charlotte Yonge among the undergraduates at Oxford was surprising as late as 1865.[15]

Miss Yonge's taste is often at its worst where a book is most vulnerable—in the title. Whatever its demerits, *The Heir of Redclyffe* is a much better novel than one would suppose from

[13] Mackail, *Life of William Morris*, I, 43. Cf. also Coleridge, *Charlotte Mary Yonge*, 183.

[14] *Charlotte Mary Yonge*, 65.

[15] Coleridge, *Charlotte Mary Yonge*, 183.

the spelling of -clyffe. *The Daisy Chain, or Aspirations* (1856) is even more unfortunately named. This novel deals with the family life of the Mays, who, like most of Yonge's characters, are very conscientious, almost exemplary in conduct, and yet quite real, quite personal. Their sins are usually small ones, such as the world overlooks, but here they entail punishment. There is considerable concern in this novel with specifically Anglo-Catholic interests, such as church restoration and confession. The poor people of Cocksmoor are miserable, and far from a church. Ethel May tries to establish a school among them, but the Ladies' Committee interferes. She does not want to submit to their advice, but, "if the lawful authority—if a good Clergyman would only come, how willingly would I work under him."[16] Thus the Oxford Movement is becoming a part of ordinary life.

The later novels of Yonge are inferior to the two I have mentioned. In *Hopes and Fears; or, Scenes from the Life of a Spinster* (1860), one of the most important figures is an Anglo-Catholic curate, Robert Fulmort, who tries to atone for the evil his family is perpetrating with its gin palaces. He undergoes persecution at the hands of mobs stimulated by the Fulmort firm and their gin. This is witness to that growing interest in social work which the novels show us taking place in the Oxford Movement about this time.[17]

The Trial: More Links of the Daisy Chain (1864), is about the May family again, and takes us across the Atlantic, where we get an interesting contrast between the typical American and the Anglo-Catholic outlook: The American girl had been bred up to liberal religious ways, but drawn on by her friend's greater precision of religious knowledge and the beauty of the

[16] II, i, 5.
[17] See below, Ch. XIII.

Church system she became more interested in Episcopalianism. After a while, "the fuller and more systematic doctrine, and the development of the beauty and daily guidance of the Church, had softened the bright American girl, so as to render her infinitely dearer to her English friend."[18] As the first part of the title indicates, this novel employs the sensationalism of the 'sixties.[19]

The Clever Woman of the Family (1865), as the title would suggest, shows how a person who is cleverer than others may be a dupe. In this novel, Mr. Mauleverer has not taken orders because he cannot be bound by the formularies. Of course, being a Liberal, he is obviously not a gentleman and proves to be a scoundrel. But not until he has gulled the Clever Woman.

We have already gone beyond the 'fifties and the typical novel of the 'fifties. Some of Miss Yonge's later novels will be discussed in Chapter XIII.

Though there is constantly in the background of Miss Yonge's mind a deep love of Anglo-Catholicism, her novels contain little that is controversial. It is rather that her characters have their being in an Anglo-Catholic atmosphere. Even in lighter moments, thoughts of church work and Catholic literature[20] are not far from them, but in the more serious trials their faith becomes most important. When Guy is told by Mrs. Lavers that it was she who sent for the clergyman that baptized him, his face beams with gratitude. "Then I have to thank you for more than all the world besides."[21] This is Catholic faith in baptismal regeneration; but contrast the way it comes into this novel as a passing remark in the life of an Anglo-Cath-

---

[18] II, v, vi, quotation, p. 130.

[19] It will be mentioned in Part III below with reference to sensationalism.

[20] The books mentioned in *The Heir of Redclyffe* include *I Promessi Sposi, The Christian Year, Butler's Analogy, Mort d'Arthur,* and Southey.

[21] *The Heir of Redclyffe,* XXII, 280.

olic, with the direct argument that it would have occasioned in the 'forties. When Guy's birthday falls in Holy Week, there can be no rejoicing.[22] In the crisis of his anger against Philip, Guy thinks of Biblical passages, of Christ's wrongs and revilings.[23] When he is in despair, Christmas brings him out of it. He has no longer the sense of being in the power of evil. The light of the other life is beginning to shine out.[24] Easter steadies his gaze. As the week before has nerved him in the spirit of self-sacrifice, the feast day brings him true unchanging joy, help to endure the want of earthly hope.[25]

In dealing with Death, Miss Yonge garners the fine fruit of her faith, for, without ignoring human pain, she avoids theatrical sentimentality. Her steady gaze is neither averted from sorrow, nor cruelly bold.[26] She was able to meet this awful test so well because her slight genius was fortified by Christian tenderness—and Christian hope. In these scenes we have an example of a certain faith forming an element of strength in literary art.

The most important way in which Yonge and the true novel of manners reflect the Oxford Movement appears in the psychology. Beliefs about the nature of the mind often depend on religious beliefs; indeed, "psychology" can never be more than the interpretation of man in terms of some philosophy. I have suggested a relation, in Newman and Kingsley, between the author's faith and the way he portrays the workings of the mind. But, in Newman, at least, one feels that specific problems are

[22] *Ibid.*, XXIV, 310.
[23] *Ibid.*, XVI, 216-217.
[24] *Ibid.*, XXII, 282-284.
[25] *Ibid.*, XXIV, 313.
[26] E.g. the death of the mother at the beginning of *The Daisy Chain;* Guy's death; or *The Pillars of the House,* I, iv.

set and then characters constructed to illustrate them. Miss
Yonge's figures are alive in their own right. They are human
beings. But she shows that human beings react in certain ways,
that their minds have certain laws, that certain consequences
spring from the very structure of reality. And often her interpretations are determined by Anglo-Catholic views. We have
seen how Paget or Gresley would build a story to illustrate
dogma. But Miss Yonge does not do this. The Movement
comes into her stories more subtly, though perhaps even more
potently. Guy Morville is conscious of a strength not his own
to resist his passionate nature.[27] This translates into common
terms of fiction a belief in the Grace of God overcoming Original Sin. Perhaps the most remarkable thing about the Tractarians was the way they combined a Romantic reverence for
external nature with a great contempt for the natural instincts.
Guy thinks it profane for a man like Byron to interpret nature.
He says, that "there is danger in listening to a man who is
sure to misunderstand the voice of nature,—danger, lest by
filling our ears with the wrong voice we should close them to
the true one. I should think there was a great chance of being
led to stop short at the material beauty, or worse, to link human passions with the glories of nature, and to distort, defile,
profane them." It is safe to read Scott's and Wordsworth's de-
scriptions of nature because they had religion.[28] (Contrast this
orthodox condemnation of Man as he is naturally, with the

---

[27] *The Heir of Redclyffe*, V, 74.

[28] XXX, 384-5. Somewhat similarly Agellius in *Callista* says, "Oh that
I did not find the taint of the city in these works of God! Alas! sweet
Nature, the child of the Almighty, is made to do the fiend's work, and
does it better than the town [as a place for revelry]. O, ye beautiful trees
and fair flowers, O bright sun and balmy air, what a bondage ye are in,
and how ye groan till you are redeemed from it! Ye are bond-slaves, but
not willingly, as man is. . . ." *Callista*, I, 11.

liberalism of Kingsley, or with the whole current away from Catholicism from the Renaissance to the Freudian generation.)

The devotion of Miss Yonge's characters to doing good (particularly in furthering religious practices) is well within the tradition of Catholicism, with its emphasis on works. And their minute conscientiousness is characteristic of a faith where the smaller details of worship are carefully observed. The Puritan conscience is stern, but it is concentrated on a few matters, just as the Puritan religion is what the Catholic calls "impoverished," dispensing with a large part of Christian culture.[29] Particularly Tractarian is Miss Yonge's belief in obedience almost for the sake of obedience, and in the evil consequences of self-will. She glorifies submission, not only to the Church, but to any misfortune, for the latter she considers particularly the will of God. The application is often psychological; Laura's agony, upon hearing that Philip was sick, was untempered by resignation, as it was uncheered by prayer.[30] Our attention is fixed not on Anglo-Catholic principles, but upon the moral choice to be guided by those principles, and upon the misery destined as a punishment for any moral heresy. The Clever Woman of the Family is punished for listening to a Liberal. In *The Three Brides*,[31] one bride is punished for her secularity. In *The Daisy Chain*, Flora May has worldly ambitions, and marries a man for his wealth and social position. This leads, with the coöperation of accidents, to the death of their child, through the error of a nurse wanting in "any high religious principle to teach her obedience or sincerity."[32] The mother, who, by her own neglect, has been ultimately responsible, is in despair. She sees that, though she seemed to herself

[29] Cf., the quotation above in Chapter VIII (p. 85), from *Villette*.

[30] *The Heir of Redclyffe*, XXXIV, 426.
[31] See below, Ch. XIII.
[32] II, xx, 228.

to be trying to do right, it was all hollow, and for the sake of praise.[33]

> The simplicity and hearty piety which, with all Dr. May's faults, had always been part of his character, and had borne him, in faith and trust, through all his trials, had never belonged to her. Where he had been sincere, erring only from impulsiveness, she had been double-minded and calculating; and, now that her delusion had been broken down, she had nothing to rest upon. Her whole religious life had been mechanical, deceiving herself more than even others, and all seemed now swept away.[34]

But while a novel of controversy can be analyzed, and a novel of plot outlined, a novel of manners must be read.

Miss Yonge is a real artist in this sense: What she sets for herself to do she does so well that as we read we are seldom conscious of any flaw, omission or blunder. Her style is quiet and pleasant, as the above quotation illustrates. Her humor is sweet and sound. Dialogue is very natural, and in itself develops the story. Like the majority of great novelists, she uses the dramatic method. Most important of all, her primary object is to tell a story of domestic life, and a story in which character is of much more interest than plot. But she is sentimental and her range of vision small. For all her merits, and her insight into psychological subtleties, Miss Yonge never touches profound experience or the exalted heights of the spirit. She did not have the necessary intellect, passion, or nobility. Her religion is not mysticism, but church-going raised to the nth degree She does not take us into the world of ideas nor of great events, but of personal domestic feeling. It is this that distinguishes the novel of manners in the 'fifties from that which was to come later.

We may point out that there is a long line of development

[33] II, xx, 223.
[34] II, xx, 224.

for serious-minded fiction from the controversial tales pro-
posing specific measures in the 'forties, through novels like
those of Charlotte Yonge, Mrs. Gaskell, and Elizabeth Sewell,
concerned with tracing minutely the consequences of moral
acts, to George Eliot. And even Eliot is merely a link between
the social and psychological studies of the earlier period and
the "philosophic romance" and naturalistic fiction of the end of
the century. No one could be more interested in the life of
society as a body than were Gresley, Kingsley, and Heygate,
more interested in the inner workings of the mind than Newman, more interested in moral consequences than Miss Yonge
or Miss Sewell. In the latter's *Cleve Hall,* a rector says that
seemingly trifling offences, if committed wilfully, and against
warning, bring upon us irremediable punishment.[35]

But why should this type of fiction, at least where our
thread brings us into contact with it, take, in the 'fifties, the
form of novel of manners? In the 'forties, the fight was over
doctrines. But the difference between Catholic Yonge and Protestant Brontë is one of ethics. As we pass from the early
Disraeli, through Kingsley to Trollope, we pass from advocacy
of theory to the photographing of social conduct,—not without
the moral implications which Poetic Justice can preach. And
technique accommodates itself to this development. Argumentative dialogue is replaced by life itself moulded into artistic
shape. Women novelists make great contributions to the new
domestic form. As one of the possible causes of the change, I
have suggested the growing power of Liberalism, since this
was a philosophy that did not agree to accept any quotable
formulae, and tried to respect nothing but human instinct and
observable phenomena. Even the Anglo-Catholic novelists of
the 'fifties turned their attention in the same direction. Another

[35] XXXII, 273.

cause, undoubtedly, within the specific subject of portrayal of the Oxford Movement, was that there had been enough time for a generation to grow up in Tractarian homes; it was now possible to present realistic pictures of domestic manners shot through with Anglo-Catholicism, for such domestic manners now existed. Fiction recommending the Anglo-Catholic way of life need not confine itself to the proposal of revolutionary principles. Let us allow a third cause in the shifts of fictional fashions that sheer demand for novelty could produce. But the fourth cause is probably the real underlying reason: England had passed from the "hungry 'forties" to the "prosperous 'fifties." The repeal of the Corn Laws (1846) had not been followed by the disasters prophesied. The discoveries in California and Australia led to an increase in the world's supply of gold. The landed aristocracy continued in wealth. The manufacturers were increasing their exports. And the condition of the laboring classes began to improve. No one had known what would be the result of Chartist agitation, but, in 1848, the Chartists made their last attempt to influence the government, and definitely failed. With the fear of revolution gone, turmoil and class conflict dying down, with even the Crimean War to dampen dissension at home, it is natural that the emphasis in fiction should shift from a controversial, sometimes melodramatic, treatment of all kinds of programs and social problems, to a study of the details of living, a kindly attention to local and domestic society, and to the ambitions or loves of individuals, who are now real personalities. Economics and politics, as well as theology, may account for variations within the art of fiction.

CHAPTER XI

THE CRUSADE AGAINST INTELLECT,
LOWER LEVELS

THE Renaissance and Reformation served to free the reason, to liberate the individual from tradition, to undermine all sorts of external authority. The French Revolution and the rise of science and scholarship (Biblical criticism, Church history) carried the world several steps farther towards accepting the individual reason as the measure of all things. In *Hopes and Fears* Charlotte Yonge indicates that the Liberals conquered English culture around the middle of the century, for she contrasts those who had fed on "Scott, Wordsworth, and Fouqué, took their theology from the *British Critic,* and their taste from Pugin; and moulded their opinions and practice on the past" with "the new generation, that of Kingsley, Tennyson, Ruskin, and the *Saturday Review.* Chivalry had given way to common sense, romance to realism, respect for antiquity to pitying patronage, the past to the future. Perhaps the present has lost in reverence and refinement as much as it has gained in clearness and confidence."[1] As we have pointed out, the Catholic Revival was an avowed reaction against this whole stream of Liberalism and Rationalism. One of the great attempts of genius to establish something besides the unassisted intellect as a means of reaching truth was *An Essay in Aid of a Grammar of Assent*, by Newman. His vivid

[1] II, xv, 281.

distrust of human reason we have already seen in his novels. But Newman's own conversion inspired in some of the Tractarians an additional fear of intelligence. If excessive intellectual activity by any chance did not lead to scepticism and democratic sentiments, it might lead to Rome. So fine a mind as Newman's could not save him from error. Perhaps it was better not to have a fine mind. By taking the position that blind obedience is the supreme virtue, the Puseyite novelists were able to defend themselves from both of their most dangerous enemies at once. In so far as they fought at all, the advocates of Anglo-Catholicism who wrote novels of manners were much more interested in carrying on this warfare against private judgment than in baiting mere Protestants. In the 'fifties they did this not so much by direct argument as by passing comment or by outcome of events. I have indicated, by analyzing the method of one author, the form which Tractarian fiction took after it passed the stage of the openly controversial novel. But prejudice and occasional preaching were far from dead. We may now look at the attack on intellect, and the praise of submission to authority, that we find incorporated into the fiction of Miss Yonge, and of two other novelists who are interesting chiefly for their anti-intellectualism. It will be noticed that the fray is still the same one that we were watching in the first two chapters of this part, but that we are now on the other side of the battle-line.

I have already mentioned *The Clever Woman of the Family* and Miss Yonge's effort to ridicule the type of person designated by the title. Her suspicion of intellect is very strong. In *The Daisy Chain* one of the best of curates is represented as not very brilliant. Another young man, Norman May, is first addicted to pride of intellect, but that goes. At one time he had his doubts, but probably believed all the time, with his heart.

Ethel, his sister, says she supposes examination was right, for a man, but she would only have tried to pray the terrible thought away. Norman does not know how far his doubt was a sin, but hopes to be forgiven for it, and he wishes to leave this world of argument where devotion is lost. (He becomes a Missionary.) Their father is indignant at his having meddled with those accursed books, and after this is "inclined to hold poor Oxford in horror."[2] Of Miss Yonge, her biographer tells us, "People who 'argued' might easily be lost, and when she wished to represent a heroine as being tempted to 'Romanize,' she says that she must be careful not to realize her difficulties for fear of becoming confused herself,"—though Keble did not seem to take this view with regard to so clever a woman.[3] In *Hopes and Fears* a girl who had been taught not to believe in such things as Hell, finally learns better, and feels such horror for intelligence that, hearing her idiot sister croon an infant school ditty, she says, "Oh! to be as silly as she is!"[4]

Next to Charlotte Yonge, the greatest Anglo-Catholic novelist before Shorthouse was Elizabeth Missing Sewell. Her best novels, unlike those of most authors, were neither definitely "for the young" nor did they openly invite the attention of grown men; they were "for young ladies," a class (of fiction) which we do not have today. At once adult in taste and language, juvenile in morality and experience, they are pictures of manners too serious for us to ignore. We must treat these borderline works, though we need not overstep the limits of adult interest so far as to include the distinctively juvenile tales *Amy Herbert* and *Laneton Parsonage*.

[2] II, xvi, 170f.
[3] Coleridge, *Charlotte Mary Yonge*, 169.
[4] II, ix, 180-182.

Miss Sewell lived nearly a century on the Isle of Wight. She was indoctrinated with Tractarianism by her brother,[5] the William Sewell who wrote *Hawkstone* and burned Froude's *Nemesis of Faith*. In her we get the extreme manifestation of one element in the Oxford Movement, for her special function seems to have been the use of Anglo-Catholic doctrines to keep women and children mentally obedient. Perhaps with women just beginning to demand freedom it was all the more necessary to concentrate the fire on that sector, and staunchly defy what was beyond doubt the wickedest tenet of Liberalism. Let us first glance briefly at the individual novels.

Gertrude (1845) is one of the earliest of genuine stories infused with elements from Anglo-Catholicism. It is connected with the Oxford Movement, chiefly through its interest in church building. It is not a clerical novel, nor on the other hand is it a love story. Gertrude Courtenay is a woman with a magic personal influence, because she has an unceasing remembrance of God. We have an illustration of the extreme tenderness of conscience which marks the characters of Miss Yonge and Miss Sewell when Gertrude hesitates to give money from her small income to build a church, because the act would bring her so much pleasure. Perhaps she should give away her money differently now, to things that would be greater sacrifices, and wait until she has lived longer, suffered more, and learned to be better, before permitting herself the indulgence of giving as she wishes to.[6] One is reminded of the writer's childhood fancy that every time the thought of a vow came into her head she had actually made it, and was bound to keep it. "I even went so far as to worry myself with the question whether

[5] *Autobiography*, 57.
[6] XXVIII, 180-181.

I was not bound to kill my mother, because I thought I had made a vow that I would."[7] When Gertrude, because of her brother's debts, could no longer consider the building of the church her duty, Mr. Dacre suggested that he himself give the money for it. Gertrude turned away. That was a bitter moment, never remembered without penitence, for she had believed that her will was subdued.[8] Humility and consciousness of the need of grace appear in Gertrude's telling another that we have but to ask for strength and receive it. The power to do right cannot be obtained by our own efforts.[9] Gertrude is devoted, calm, unmarried—a sort of secular nun.

Margaret Percival (1847) is entirely different, and much more like the novels by other Anglo-Catholics in the 'forties, for it is openly controversial, with elaborate discussion of doctrine. The Oxford Movement had received such a check from secessions to Rome that her brother William urged her to write something pointing out to young people the true claims of the English Church.[10] It does not occur to Margaret to wonder if she is entering on a safe path in allowing herself to become a friend of the Countess Novera, a woman of higher rank and a Roman Catholic. Father Andrea sets out to convert her. Dangerously ignorant of Church history, "She conceded, without difficulty, the title of Catholic [to the Romanists]; talked of the Established Church of England and the Established Church of Scotland in the same terms; she even once spoke of a person, whose name was casually mentioned, as a Unitarian Clergyman."[11]

[7] *Autobiography*, 24-25.
[8] *Gertrude*, XXXIV, 239.
[9] XXX, 208-209.
[10] *Autobiography*, 99.
[11] I, xxiv, 178.

The right of private judgement is much spoken of, and supposed to be a great privilege; but there are not many, especially among women, who find it so. Their very physical weakness makes them willing to be governed, especially in questions of religion; and it is this way that a power which comes before them, speaking authoritatively and requiring unreserved submission, seizes upon their imagination, and easily triumphs over their reason. Superiority of intellect is no safeguard; for the minds which think the most, have the greatest perception of the awfulness and mysteriousness of life, and the greatest longing for rest.[12]

Fortunately Margaret's practical duties keep her from thinking too much. And she is saved by her uncle, a High Church clergyman, Mr. Sutherland, who sees "the imminent danger to which Margaret would be exposed if she once allowed herself to believe that the change of religion was a question of conscience and feeling only."[13] He says that the conscience is a safe guide only if it agrees with the revelation and law that God has given us.[14] Margaret had perhaps been unable to perceive truth because she lacked "humility—the willingness to obey an authority set over her, although it did not entirely accord with her own ideas." Mr. Sutherland speaks of "the duty of remaining where God has placed you, unless you have absolute demonstration, which you never can have, that the English Church is no true Church."[15] And he suggests that Margaret will go to Hell if she does what is right in her own eyes and examines the claims of Rome.[16] Intercourse with the Countess must cease. Margaret sees that she must seek for guidance as to whether the Church of England is a true Church only from

[12] I, xxviii, 228-229.
[13] II, xxiv, 162.
[14] II, xxxi, 216.
[15] II, xxiv.
[16] II, xxxi.

clergymen of the Church of England.[17] In the end she is freed
of doubt by the steady avoidance of controversy. There is no
love story connected with this heroine, except that of her "humble, trusting, reverential, absorbing love"[18] for the Countess,
marred as it is by religious obstacles and a triangle situation
of jealousy over a third woman. So far as we know, Margaret
never sees or is seen by a young man. The story is primarily
one of a religious quest. Should she join Rome? And yet it is
dramatic. Again theological propositions have been translated
into flesh—if that word may be used without impropriety when
speaking of Mid-Victorian maidens and countesses.

The Experience of Life (1852) is a peculiar title for a novel
telling of a maiden lady and her efforts to support her mother.
She finds her true home in the Church, where she goes morning and evening for worship.[19]

The preface to *Katherine Ashton* (1854) says that the object is to describe what actually is. As to the best mode of caring
for the poor, until it is determined by competent authority, "it
would seem safer and wiser, for women at least, to take advantage of the machinery placed within their reach, than to
criticize its defects, and speculate upon the means of its improvement." District societies and a clergyman's wife may be
less valuable than sisterhoods, but if we wait until we decide
which is best opportunities of usefulness will be lost. The
novel does not refer much to Anglo-Catholicism, even with regard to the clergyman, Reeves, who appears in it frequently.
But it shows favorably one who is content to do her duty in
the station to which God has called her, and not be a social
climber. Mr. Reeve's wife says that only Church education will

[17] II, xli.
[18] II, xxv, 177, Margaret writing to "Beatrice" (the Countess).
[19] II, xxii.

raise the tone of society without making people want to go out of their sphere. Distinctions of rank would exist even if all people were well-bred, for God has appointed them. They are fully recognized in the Bible.[20]

Ivors (1856) illustrates the development of the novel towards more emphasis on plot. It was, Sewell says in her *Autobiography,* "my first attempt at a regular novel, or a story in which love is the essential interest." (A definition that agrees with that implied by earlier Tractarian novelists.) Up to that time she had tried to show life important and happy apart from marriage.[21] This novel contains an amusing strong-minded woman, Lady Augusta Clare, bent on educating her stepdaughter in simplicity and ignorance of evil. This is an excellent satire on moral snobbery. *Ursula* (1858) gives a realistic picture of country life, a story in which a conscience again tenderly and minutely weighs right and wrong in the scale of obedience. The heroine marries in the end.

In these novels is expressed perhaps the most extreme scorn for intellect to be found in all Victorian literature. In *Gertrude* the heroine says her notions about the Church began from practice. A friend talked to her about the duty of observing certain days, and attending daily services;

> she was not at all a clever person, and understood nothing of controversy, but she was most entirely in earnest, and never, that I could find out, knowingly omitted a duty; and all her argument was, that fasts and festivals were ordered, and that there was a form of daily service in the prayer-book which the clergyman of the parish intended to use; and she asked me whether I thought we were at liberty to follow our notions of right, rather than obey the rules of the Church.

[20] II, xlii.
[21] *Autobiography,* 145.

Gertrude's sister Edith says that she could hardly have listened to the arguments of one whose judgment she did not respect. Gertrude answers that since this friend's knowledge of duty was not the result of human reasoning, it seemed to claim more reverence.[22] In her *Autobiography,* Miss Sewell has told that as a schoolgirl she was full of sceptical thoughts. At last she resolved to crush them. "This was done by a short quick prayer, and an almost physical effort to turn away from the suggestions." There was no trial in after life equal to that which these phantoms brought, the sense of guilt, the sense of not being forgiven. "I have sat in the drawing-room at Camden Place practising my music mechanically, whilst reasoning upon the probability of the Jewish miracles till I was nearly wild. And I had no one to turn to."[23] It is not difficult to believe that this terrible struggle to crush the freedom of her mind left its mark on her later work, perhaps even produced that homely strength which makes her personality rather impressive. Under "Extracts from The Journal 1845-48" in her *Autobiography,* she said a sermon of Newman's which she was reading would be a great safeguard against being led into mischief (by the notion of Newman himself being ready to secede): " 'Obedience, the remedy for religious perplexity.' It is an immense comfort to have one's days so occupied as to leave little time for abstract thought."[24] We have seen how *Margaret Percival* uses this principle as an argument for remaining in the English Church.

The war against dangerous intellectual activity is akin to the war against self-will of all kinds. As Mr. Dacre says, "The highest of all principles . . . is surely obedience."[25] Obedience

[22] XXVII, 176-177.
[23] 38-39.
[24] 119.
[25] *Gertrude,* XIX.

to what? Not merely to constituted authorities, but to whatever is, including all sorts of chance situations. Miss Sewell argues against putting what one thinks best above intervening obstacles. In *Ursula,* Mrs. Weir, having learned submission under the hard discipline of Mrs. Temple, though her intellect was weakened, still had full comprehension on the one subject of religion, and would say no matter what was sent, she would take it. "God sends it." This, Ursula says, was not like common sense, yet it seemed to belong to some sense that was higher and better.[26] Sometimes Miss Sewell's interpretation of religion makes it primarily that which is opposite to pride.[27] Any happening, especially an evil one, may be called the will of God, and it is particularly wicked to struggle impiously against such adversity. It is the will of God that the gambling of one brother forces another to give up his education for the Church.[28] George would not be justified in borrowing money for the purpose of continuing in the University a few years to prepare for his profession, because obstacles indicate that it is not his part in life to be a clergyman. "We must learn to act upon faith, and read the will of God in outward circumstances."[29] The gloomy duty of passive submission to the easiest course (though it may ruin one's life) is holier than the individualistic pride of following the dictates of conscience. Of course, no amount of torment by a husband can justify a wife in leaving him.[30] If there are difficulties in the way, neglect of public service becomes sanctified as obedience to Providence, or doing your duty in that station of life to which it has pleased God to call you. Mr. Dacre points out to Edward Courtenay

[26] II, lxviii. Cf. also I, xxviii.
[27] E.g., *Ursula,* I, xxxvii, 272; lxxiv, 249.
[28] *Margaret Percival,* II, xxvii, 190.
[29] *Ibid.,* II, xxix.
[30] *Ibid.,* II, xxxvi.

that if a man does not have an outward call (that is, a large income), God has not meant him to be an M.P.[31] In the end, Edward says that in running for Parliament he made his duty suit his will, instead of suiting his will to his duty. His wife asks how he could have known his duty. "External circumstances—property—my own debts."[32] Similarly, never undertake a responsibility which does not belong to you. That is one of the roots of trouble in *Ursula*. In *The Experience of Life* we are told that "When we have taken care of the relations whom God has given us, then is the time to begin to think of forming new ones of our own."[33] Marriage and charities must be put aside if they interfere with the first duty of seeing that each member of the family has a genteel livelihood,[34] Miss Sewell's idea of "nothing but the necessaries of life" being "two servants, no carriages, no luxuries."[35]

Her faith condemns conscience to abdicate in favor of legal decree. Margaret Percival did not realize the error of praising instead of reverencing the Prayer Book, for

she did not see that she was placing herself in a wrong position with regard to the Church; the position of a child, who obeys his parents because they are kind to him, and try to teach him what is right, and not because the imperative law of God has said, "Honor thy father and thy mother," [and moreover] the obedience due to the object of our own choice is but another word for obedience to our individual will; and the Bible does not say, "Let every soul be subject to the higher powers, because they are good and holy, and approve themselves to our conscience;" but it gives the injunction broadly, strongly, without definition or limitation,

[31] *Gertrude*, XIX, 127-128.
[32] *Ibid.*, XLVI, 317.
[33] II, vi, 91.
[34] *Ibid.*, 101.
[35] *Gertrude*, XLVIII, 325.

to teach us that subjection to law, fixed and unchangeable, is the
condition [of man's happiness and his hope of blessedness].[36]

Opposition to the whole tenor of Classical and Renaissance
Humanism, and to modern Liberalism, could hardly be more
extreme. Elsewhere we are told that to think Christianity made
its way into the heathen world by the holy lives of its first
teachers is a serious mistake and serious in its consequences.
"Christianity made its way in the heathen world by external
witness, by miracles, and testimony . . . by holiness as a cor-
roborative testimony, but as nothing more."[37] Miss Sewell's
preference for strength which cannot be understood or justified
on the grounds of human value appears in the way Ursula likes
to watch thunder storms. The spectacle of the vast Power
raised her thoughts above the earth. It was as if she were permitted to draw near and watch the wonderful workings of
God's wisdom.[38]

While Miss Sewell's rebellion against nineteenth-century in-
dividualism, and against the use of the reason as ultimate
judge, gives her an important place within the reaction towards
discipline, her fiction is more than its message. If there had not
been Miss Yonge, I should have chosen this writer's work to
illustrate the novel of manners. In general, what we said of
Miss Yonge's method applies to her fellow. The title-page of
Gertrude quotes from *The Excursion.*

> Turn to private life
> And social neighborhood; look we to ourselves,
> A light of duty shines on every day
> For all

[36] *Margaret Percival*, I, xxvi, 200.
[37] *The Experience of Life*, XXI, 278-279.
[38] *Ursula*, I, xlii, 304.

Nothing could better express what Miss Yonge and Miss Sewell do with the Oxford Movement. Miss Sewell gives dramatic value to religious qualities, making the reader hope for their appearance in a crisis. This is real moral conflict, *motives* set in play one against another. The obstacles are not external, but lie in flaws of character. For example, the complications of *Margaret Percival* grow out of a too great imaginative sensibility in the heroine. The author has the one great talent: she can create character, however narrow the range and shallow the depth.

Her characters and their fates demonstrate several psychological principles drawn from her religious beliefs, chiefly the necessity of obedience and the duty of not thinking for oneself. But there is also opposition to the extreme (to her, Romish) practices of confession, absolution, and minute spiritual guidance. Her women are not responsible for what they believe, but they are responsible for their conduct, and Sewell shows repugnance for the removal of all self-reproach by assurance of forgiveness.[39] The Church can tell them what to think, but cannot declare their sins forgiven. Thus we have in her religion the rigidities of a Catholic system, without its ease. The same conception of moral responsibility, that gloomiest, noblest doctrine of Puritanism, appears in Eliot's novels, there accompanied by much of the deterministic fatality—but none of the moral release—opened up by science. These Mid-Victorian women were able to draw eclectically on various philosophies, rejecting only the amenities.

There are other ways besides Miss Sewell's of attempting to crush unruly independence of thought or reliance on intellect. One of these is the exaltation of fervid emotion. Contrary to the usual belief, the Oxford Movement, in its reaction against

[39] *Margaret Percival,* II, xvi, 104.

Rationalism, was less mystical than "Fundamentalist."[40] Tomes and tomes of Tractarian writings were devoted to a defense of Catholic practices and dogmas by quotation from the Bible, while, on the other hand, until secular literature itself began to be tinged with mysticism (in a general movement at the end of the century) it is hard to find in Anglo-Catholic novels any emphasis on direct communication with the Divine. Catholic Truth is proved by detailed argument, refutation of Protestant "error," or by simple assertion and the manipulation of plot. Though there is a violent attack upon intellect as a judge of truth, the substitutes are usually custom, external institutional authority, and feeling—not the feeling of being led by the voice of God, *in spite of* external evidence. Some of our present-day misinterpretation arises from the fact that Newman was the greatest leader of the Movement. But Newman, after all, moved on out, and cannot be considered, at least in this respect, a representative spokesman. With these qualifications, however, we may recognize in the sacramental system and in the Tractarian's multiform opposition to mere intellect, potentialities of mysticism which in certain types of character, or under future influences, might produce a vivid feeling of individual union with the Divine. I have found one novel of the common-sense 'fifties that is incandescent with impassioned religious enthusiasm: Felicia Mary Francis Skene's *S. Alban's; or, the Prisoners of Hope* (1853). If not the work of a mystic, it at least goes farther than most novels of the period in capitalizing the Tractarian revival of supernaturalism. With the story of a girl's ecstatic sacramental worship it couples an assault on political and economic disobedience, thus dealing a double blow against Rationalism and its brood.

[40] Cf. *Ursula*, XXX, 230. Ursula referred to the Bible on a certain point. She knew "it was safer to follow God's hints than men's reasons."

The Vicar of S. Albans, Mr. Chesterfield, a man of good fortune, prefers to bury himself in a wretched parish and work night and day among the poor.[41] The church has been restored, so that it now has low open seats, a scarcely discernible pulpit, and costly work around the altar. Maude Elliston, who has never been taught Catholicism, sees people leaving this church, and perceives that they are knit together in a friendship she does not share. So "she laid her head upon her hands and wept." She enters the church alone, but does not feel alone. As her eyes wander to the chancel, a fear takes possession of her as if an awful Presence were there. There is a sort of atmosphere about the altar is if the latter were very awful and very holy. (As yet she knows nothing of the Sacraments.) The east window and rich altar cloth arouse feelings of reverence. She is constrained to kneel and worship.[42] Maude's brother Henry has been attending a Mechanics' Institute,[43] where he hears a lecture on the rights of man, and civil and religious liberty. He recommends Carlyle. Maude knows nothing of these books that have carried such a pernicious influence with them, but she is "instinctively" conscious that there is something wrong in

[41] X, 175.

[42] II.

[43] The Mechanics' Institutes were educational organizations looked upon with suspicion by the Tractarians. This novel calls the Institute "a society which wholly ignores the Church, and which she on her part utterly repudiates as possessing no authority from her, and being, in fact, a mere vehicle for the transmission of heretical doctrine." (IV, 66) The Mechanics' Institutes were voluntary organizations of mechanics who wished to acquire scientific knowledge. In them democratic ideas seem to have been rife. In Charlotte Yonge's *Abbeychurch or Self-Control and Self-Conceit* (1844) three girls go to a Mechanics' Institute lecture, although, as daughters of clergymen, their presence will give some sanction to the system. One bad consequence of their folly appears very soon—Fido has drowned while they were there. (VIII; X)

these new notions.[44] Henry now lies to get off early from work. This is

one of the symptoms of the great change which has been working in him ever since he joined the Mechanics' Institute. Previous to that unfortunate step he has possessed some vague notion of a duty which he had to perform to his master, on the grounds that he was bound to return him a fair amount of work, and hearty zeal, for the money he received; but his new associates had taught him to view the matter in a very different light; the manufacturer was a tyrant, a usurper, a retainer of wealth, to which he had no claim, albeit it was gained by his own industry; one of those to be put down, crushed, and beggared, in the day of retribution, to which the disaffected look with such firm hope . . . they were all equal, and men were not to be bought and sold like slaves, whose labour was to be made use of; and all this wicked sophistry being remarkably palatable to the proud unchastened spirit of the man [caused him to shirk his duties].[45]

The lecturer at the Mechanics' Institute, King, was "one of those fierce, lawless spirits, who, having wilfully flung off all authority, Divine and human, are converted, as if in mockery, by the master of all Evil, into his own most abject slaves." Though he declaims so loudly against distinctions of rank, he has no other end in view but to exalt himself, by bringing those who are his superiors down to his own level, or below it, for the principles of his party tend to raise "the people" above the aristocracy, rather than to produce a genuine equality. These "false and destructive tenets of liberalism" are well known. King is looking for an instrument to turn into a Chartist agitator, and selects Henry.[46] Henry's "intercourse with the liberals had not so completely quenched all idea of honour in his mind"

[44] III.
[45] IV, 64.
[46] IV, 65, 66.

that he yet contemplated breach of promise towards his Nelly (a factory girl), "or rather, we should say, that the seeds of baptismal grace, never fostered, Alas! by sacraments . . . yet worked with a gentle influence on that poor, darkened spirit." But King, emissary of Satan, is at hand to stifle these better promptings.[47]

But let us rise from this plane of industrial, scientific, democratic phenomena, to the supernatural level. Maude enters the church, this time when the "sacrifice of the most Holy Eucharist" is being celebrated. She drinks in every word.

> a holy terror, and an awe most sweet, though solemn, deepened and deepened in her soul, as that highest act of worship rose step by step to the crowning point of incomprehensible condescension, when the most blessed sentence that ever is uttered in mortal ears came thrilling to hers with a sudden power, and the uplifted hands and voice of the Priest proclaimed, "This is My Body," "this is My Blood." Then it was almost as though she had been struck by lightning . . . [She sank prostrate] . . . Maude was utterly ignorant of the meaning of all that had been done, but that which smote her inmost spirit with such exceeding power, was the simple conviction that those words—the words of eternal life—WERE TRUE . . . and it is not to be wondered at if she was overpowered with the discovery, thus made for the first time, [that He comes on Earth].[48]

The vicar tells Maude to submit herself to his guidance. Her mind, unbiased by previous error, embraced at once "the fundamental truth on which our whole prospects in eternity are built." She knows she gains admission to God through union with Christ, "and that this union, so ineffable and so mysterious" is "effected by the administration of the Sacraments through the agency of an earthly priesthood. . . . So deeply was she impressed with the exceeding awfulness of that Power

[47] IV, 70.
[48] V, 91-94.

whereby the Church, yet militant here below, can call into action the mediatorial office of her Head." Nor did she "ever bow herself afar off when the August Sacrifice was on that altar, which yet she dared not to approach, without an awe-struck consciousness that even then, in union with the earthly oblation, there stood a Lamb, as it had been slain, before the throne of God!"[49] The passion and almost corporeal "mysticism" of Maude's experience is suggested by what another says to her, "I do not love our LORD as you do . . . I have not the *desire* for such a fearful closeness of intercourse with Him, as the very receiving of His Body and Blood must produce. Whilst to you it is evidently the most ineffable consummation of joy; to me, it is only dreadful; it makes me shudder to think of my helpless soul, delivered up to such unobstructed contact with the terrible GOD."[50] Maude's despondent self-examination preparatory to her first communion fills a large part of the novel, rising to an ecstatic climax at Christmas. Maude now receives the Sacrament.[51]

As a contrast to Maude's beatific advance, we are shown the sins of Henry. He tries to get rid of Nelly, and she is saved by Maude from suicide. Henry and his sister are not without their disputes, for in them the novelist is contrasting Liberalism and Catholicism. When Henry calls the vicar a Pharisee, Maude exclaims, "how dare you speak so of our LORD'S own anointed Priest." Henry says he has learned at the Mechanics' Institute "what these usurping Clergy really are . . . the black dragoons, as we call them, mounting guard over the parishes of unhappy England, to keep out all liberty of conscience and truth."[52] Maude once quoted some of Henry's democratic senti-

[49] VIII, 127-128.
[50] XII, 202.
[51] XIV.
[52] X, 164.

ments to the vicar, and asked "on what principles they were to be refuted, as she felt instinctively that they were wrong." The vicar told her that He who said, "Render unto Caesar the things that are Caesar's" had Himself ordained the different ranks of society, "and therefore, that when we failed to render honour to whom honour is due, were it only from the trades-man's daughter to the child of the gentleman, we were despis-ing the ordinance of GOD."[53] The author has informed us that Henry's elevation was to be bought by the humiliation of "those whom GOD Himself had set in high places."[54] Again we have the faith that whatever is, is right, which we have already seen in Paget, Gresley, and Miss Sewell. The Charitists get up a strike at the cotton mill, preparatory to a grand demonstration. They march down to the ground before the factory and ha-rangue about liberty and equality. When the master refuses to accede to the demands, the mill is set afire. Military are sent for. Resisting, several Chartists are killed. When Maude reaches Henry, he is dying, striken by the "hand of GOD . . . when most of his pride and arrogance were rampant in revolt against his Maker!" The vicar, however, points out God's mercy in stopping him from rushing on into a career of crime that would have wrecked his soul forever.[55] There are some natures whose great peril is the intensity of their human affections, and the worst agony is needful to them "for the destruction of the dangerous sweetness they might find in sympathies too largely given to mortal beings,"[56] Hence it does Maude good to watch her beloved brother tortured by pain. Indeed, her recently ac-quired faith adds to her suffering, for she is now afraid for his

[53] X, 173.
[54] VII, 117.
[55] XV, quotation p. 254.
[56] XVI.

soul. The vicar says that if her brother speaks of his fears of future punishment, she must not comfort him, for "penitence" must come first, and the bitter agony that is its seal.[57] But in Henry is awakened a dread, far greater than the dread of Hell, of an eternal exile from Heaven. At last he receives the Blessed Sacrament.[58]

Let us go back to the fate of Nelly, the jilted factory girl. Becoming Anglo-Catholic, she had determined she would not be Henry's wife for the whole world, since he loved not the Lord. Besides, she would be "His alone—His child—" and there was a person required at S. Albans to take care of the vestments and to help in washing the altar-linen, "such happy, beautiful work."[59] When Henry is dying, she tells him "with what sickening terror" she went again and again to the vicar to tell him the agony she felt lest she be doomed to eternal punishment for loving a mortal being too much.[60] At last

> it would seem as though she who had been so swiftly drawn, with passionate longing, to the very feet of her dear LORD, there to yield up unto His love the heart that willed to love Him only, had been made early ripe for that fuller revelation of His deathless tenderness, which death alone can open to us. [She falls forward on her face. It was ever Maude's conviction that at that moment, Nelly] had heard within her soul the cry of the Bridegroom's Coming. [She dies. Maude arranges Nelly's body so that] she lay there as in the spotless bridal robes, where with she might indeed go meetly forth to the Marriage Feast of her Heavenly Bridegroom.[61]

We will take one last glance at Maude, now in charge of the apprentices in her father's shop. She refuses to receive from

[57] XVI, 279.
[58] XVIII.
[59] XII.
[60] XVII, 288.
[61] XIX, 314-323.

them slavish toil that leaves no room for worship, but grants them half an hour a day, and festivals. They make up the latter by working on the vigils preceding! "But it must not be forgotten, that . . . Maude Elliston never trusted to her own judgment," but counted it her deepest blessing that she could flee for counsel to one who had "received none other than GOD the HOLY GHOST in Sacramental gift."[62]

Perhaps never did a novelist try to dramatize so thoroughly a religion *as such*. Everything is seen in the light of Catholicism. "It was Advent, . . . the earth, obeying that wonderful instinct of nature, which seems ever to harmonize so beautifully with the consecrated seasons of the Church's year," instinctively got snowed on "arrayed herself in a garment of snow that she might wait in spotless robes the appearance of her Sinless LORD."[63] Maude, taught by her new faith "to reverence the dead, whose consecrated remains still, by sacramental union, form part of the LORD'S Own Body;" trod lightly through the churchyard.[64] The vicar says that no authors are so pernicious as the German. Nearly all their works are either openly or covertly rationalistic. "You know all those books are essentially opposed to the Church, and the very first principle laid down in them is generally, that it is derogatory to the dignity of intellect and reason to submit itself to given laws," especially such as work through a priesthood.[65]

This is almost all we have to show in fiction for the supposed mysticism of the early Oxford Movement. It is part of that crusade against the free exercise of the mind and for unques-

[62] XIX, quotations p. 312.
[63] VIII, 126-127.
[64] VIII, 140.
[65] XVIII, 294-295.

tioning obedience to established authorities (especially to the Catholic minority of the Anglican priesthood), which is one of the most persistent features of the Tractarian novel, whether written by priests or by maiden ladies, whether in the form of direct argument or of properly colored pictures of manners.

CHAPTER XII

THE PORTRAIT BY TROLLOPE

THE period of fiction controversial in form and belligerent in tone had definitely given way to a more tolerant
portrayal of manners before Anthony Trollope's pictures of
the "Barchester" clergy began to appear. That is one reason
why his clerical fiction is so different from that of Newman
and the early Kingsley. I will offer other explanations later.

Trollope's references to the Oxford Movement are few, but
they have the merit of being well written, and they are less
biased than those of any earlier novelist. The theme of *The
Warden* (1855) would have been perfectly fitted to a Tractarian novel bent on propaganda. The illegal appropriation of
funds on the part of a clergyman comes under the sweep of
liberal reform. Our sympathy is turned all in favor of the clerical culprit who is driven from his comfortable home, for he
is a kind-hearted old man, who has simply never thought that
his position might not be right. When agitation arises, his
tender conscience and dislike of battle lead him to resign the
sinecure, much to the disgust of Archdeacon Grantly, who has
faith in the sanctity of clerical incomes. This synopsis, however, gives an entirely wrong idea of the novel, for in the story
as we read it the point in controversy seems of very little importance; we think only of the dramatic situations, and the
lovable or amusing characters. Like so many of the novels we
have discussed, it is not primarily a love story, but the story of

a man's conscience in a situation that would be likely to occur in the English Church of the early nineteenth century. And yet it is the individual, not the abstract problem, that interests the author. Perhaps for this reason there are practically no references to Tractarianism,[1] though that movement was in its beginnings a protest against just such liberal reform of Church revenue.

In *Barchester Towers* (1857) we have a fight for power on the part of a Low-Church Bishop's wife and a clergyman, Mr. Slope, whose "soul trembles in agony at the iniquities of the Puseyites."[2] The clergymen of Barchester have been High and Dry, not Puseyite: "they had no candles on their altars, either lighted or unlighted; they made no private genuflexions, and were contented to confine themselves to such ceremonial observances as had been in vogue for the last hundred years . . . chanting was confined to the cathedral, and the science of intoning was unknown." But since the Bishop and his party are very low, it behooves the leader of the opposition, Dr. Grantly, to be of the very highest. "He would not willingly alter his own fashion of dress, but he could people Barchester with young clergymen dressed in the longest frocks, and in the highest-breasted silk waistcoats. He certainly was not prepared to cross himself, or to advocate the real presence; but, without going this length, there were various observances, by adopting which he could plainly show his antipathy to such men as Dr. Proudie and Mr. Slope."[3] One of Trollope's few Puseyites appears in this novel, Mr. Arabin, who had been an ardent disciple of Newman at Oxford, and was "so high, indeed, that at one period of his career he had all but toppled over into the

[1] One of the few is in Ch. XV, p. 188.
[2] IV, 27.
[3] VI, 41-42.

cesspool of Rome."[4] He becomes a writer of Tractarian polemics.

In *Doctor Thorne* (1858), the third of the series, is introduced Mr. Oriel, who had been inoculated with very High-Church principles at Oxford. He went into orders, influenced by an enthusiastic love for the priesthood.

> But it may perhaps be said of him, without speaking slanderously, that his original calling, as a young man, was rather to the outward and visible signs of religion than to its inward and spiritual graces. He delighted in lecterns and credence-tables, in services at dark hours of winter mornings when no one would attend, . . . and in all the paraphernalia of Anglican formalities which have given such offence to those of our brethren who live in daily fear of the scarlet lady.[5]

Many were afraid that he would deliver himself over to that lady, but he was not of that stuff which is necessary for a burning, self-denying convert. Nevertheless, "certain lengths in self-privation Mr. Oriel did go; at any rate, for some time. He eschewed matrimony, imagining that it became him as a priest to do so; he fasted rigorously on Fridays;" and he was thought to scourge himself.[6] In spite of his adhesion to celibacy, a number of unmarried women of the community turned devoted Puseyites, especially Miss Gushing. But—his hostility to matrimony vanishing—Mr. Oriel found himself engaged to Miss Gresham. (From the time Miss Gushing heard of this, she became an Independent Methodist, and the credence-table covering she had been working was cut up into slippers for a preacher's feet.)[7]

[4] XIV, 107; Ch. XX.
[5] XXXII, 337-338.
[6] XXXII, 338.
[7] XXXII, 338-342.

The Barsetshire clergy appear in *Framley Parsonage* (1861), *The Small House at Allington* (1864), and even somewhat in *The Claverings* (1867), which is not of the Barchester series. *The Last Chronicle of Barset* (1867) says little of Anglo-Catholicism, but indicates that the High Church clergy no longer dance and play cards as they did formerly.[8] Mrs. Proudie, the Bishop's wife, and villainess or butt of the Barchester novels, is very Low-Church. She objects to anything that smacks of confession.[9] She "always went to church on Sunday evenings, making a point of hearing three services and three sermons every Sunday of her life. On week-days she seldom heard any, having an idea that week-day services were an invention of the High-Church enemy, and that they should therefore be vehemently discouraged. Services on saints' days she regarded as rank papacy, and had been known to accuse a clergyman's wife, to her face, of idolatry, because the poor lady had dated a letter, St. John's Eve."[10]

But these references are few, and if I had not pruned them down, they would have been repetitious. One could read all of Trollope, the greatest novelist of clerical life, without becoming aware that the Oxford Movement was of any importance in the nineteenth-century Church (though in his novels the Evangelical enemy plays a major rôle). We are met with the old question, "Is Trollope's picture reliable?" And this study has provided us with a new test. For we may compare his High Church clergymen with those of the other novelists whom we have discussed. Immediately the great difference is obvious: in Trollope's portrait, even of Anglo-Catholics, there is almost no religion. This does not merely result in stories of the

[8] I, xxii, 192-193.
[9] I, xi, 97.
[10] I, xvii, 148.

human side of clerical life; it produces the direct impression that these men were not interested in religion. It is like a "Hamlet-without-the-hero." When we are shown other motives for almost every action, we naturally conclude that enthusiasm, beliefs, theology, and the sense of supernatural duties played little part in the life of the profession he describes. Now this may have been true of the majority of Victorian High Church clergymen, but was it true of the Anglo-Catholics? In the pictures presented by Paget, Gresley, Newman, Kingsley, Yonge, Conybeare, we see participants in the Oxford Movement considering religious zeal and theological questions matters of real importance. Partisanship seems to have been more than politics, and to have grown out of real intellectual opposition. The Church was an arena not only of domestic animosities, but of religious warfare between great philosophies. All of these other novelists were close to the Movement. But Trollope himself even disclaims any special knowledge of the clergy. For "in writing about clergymen generally I had to pick up as I went whatever I might know or pretend to know about them."[11] However much we may allow for excessive modesty in the author, I do not see how we can think that Trollope alone presented the facts, and that the others were mistaken. And Trollope seems definitely to slip in his portrayal on such a detail as this: He says that Mr. Arabin, having decided not to go over to Rome, "professed himself a confirmed Protestant."[12] Would he? A High Church partisan, still "ready at a moment's notice to take up the cudgels in opposition to anything that savoured of an evangelical bearing,"[13] would he have called himself a Protestant? Other novelists

[11] *Autobiography*, 83, 84.
[12] *Barchester Towers*, **XX**, 160.
[13] *Ibid.*, 161.

show that it was one of the tenderest points with the Tractarians that the English Church be considered as Catholic as the Roman. And if Trollope had been acutely aware of this feeling, he would surely not have used "Protestant" loosely merely to mean Anglican, for his writing is marked by care for the connotation of words.

Trollope's pictures of the Victorian clergy are incomplete, and he knew it. For within the course of the novels themselves he warns us that he has not portrayed the clergy as clergymen, but only with reference to their social life.[14] Disclaimers notwithstanding, in a realistic study omission is tantamount to denial. To portray Anglo-Catholic clergymen of the Mid-Victorian age with reference only to their social life is not to portray Anglo-Catholics at all, but incomplete High and Dry Churchmen of the old type.

Trollope's Church is not a divine society, a mystical body speaking with the voice of God. It is not holy. It is a bureau of state. Its ministers are like civil service officials translated into clergymen. He said, "I costumed and styled my people ecclesiastically for the sake of novelty. Beyond that I never intended my clerical portraiture to go."[15] Most of his clergy are neither Low nor Tractarian nor Broad; they are the old High and Dry Orthodox, as he himself remarks.[16] They are the fox-hunting parsons, de-foxed as far as Victorian taste required.[17] There may have been a large number of such charming worldly clergymen in Trollope's day, but in so far as we are left with the impression that they constituted all of the "High Church"

[14] *Framley Parsonage*, XLII, 407; *The Last Chronicle of Barset*, Il, lxxxiv, 387-388.

[15] Escott, *Anthony Trollope*, 112.

[16] *Barchester Towers*, VI, 45.

[17] *The Last Chronicle of Barset*, II, lviii, 151; *The Claverings*, II, 15; the career of Mark Roberts in *Framley Parsonage*.

according to the meaning of the word in the 'fifties, Trollope's
picture is false. And there is in the total effect more than a
suspicion of anachronism. We have been going through a generation of novels, and the picture of the clergy has gradually
changed. The Tractarians have crept in, then raised a disturb-
ance, then settled down in good livings. The Broad Churchmen
have come up from below, dressed like "socialists." Evangelicals have retreated farther and farther into the background, but
remain entrenched behind a good generation of impressive respectability. Then suddenly Trollope sweeps us back to the
dawn. Again the High Churchmen are staunch Protestants.
Liberalism is a governmental bother. The Evangelicals are vul-
garians trying unsuccessfully to intrude into a fold reserved
for gentlemen.[18] We have seen such a clerical world before—in
The Vicar of Wrexhill, by Trollope's mother. Though Anthony
places his novels in his own day, and tells us that Newman has
gone over to Rome, he is really saying little that would not
have applied equally well to the preceding generation. He is
carrying on the family tradition. Indeed, he tells us that he inherited some of his mother's antipathies towards the Evangelical school, and speaks of his Mr. Slope as "the unbeneficed
descendant of my mother's Vicar of Wrexhill."[19] Archdeacon
Grantly, Escott says, was Mrs. Trollope's father. "As his
youthful guest, the author of *Barchester Towers* had been introduced to clerical life on its social side, and had observed
the personal germs that afterwards grew into the Warden, Mr.
Harding, and Dean Arabin."[20] This does not necessarily vitiate
completely Trollope's picture of the Oxford Movement, in so
fas as he noticed it at all. He probably portrayed what he saw

[18] *Barchester Towers,* VIII, 55; VI, 40-41.
[19] Escott, *Anthony Trollope,* 111-112.
[20] *Ibid.,* 205.

—but his sight was not profound. We may discount particularly, as a concession to Mid-Victorian sentimentality, the cant of poor-celibate-but-you-will-marry-the-first-fair-woman-who-wants-you, in more modern parlance, the we're-all-humans-after-all strain. There is nothing more insulting to an idealist than to tolerate him because he really doesn't mean it.

We have indicated some of the ties between religion and technique in the novels of Newman, Kingsley and Yonge. Does Trollope's art correspond in any sense to his own preference for the High and Dry religion? It does. The style is mild, urbane, humorous, unenthusiastic—capable of suggesting subtle gradations in social rank, but not of achieving the sublime. Characterization is undogmatic. People—of cultivation—are interesting for themselves, and as representatives of highly civilized society, or as its enemies. They do not typify any other cause, less so even than in the liberal novels. Trollope's is a conservative realism. It is difficult to believe that he was contemporary with Reade and Eliot, or that half the Barchester series appeared later than *The Ordeal of Richard Feverel*! Setting and character are still not fused, as they are soon to be by the determinists. As an artist, Trollope shows a genius for grasping the concrete reality, and for accepting it with a pleasant smile. Above all things, he loves to give us the atmosphere of groups and parties. He is very tolerant of snobbery. He is delicately conscious of the implications of class, and he conveys this consciousness to the reader with perfect skill. All of this is distinctly the art suitable to a gentleman who would consider it bad taste to be a saint.

Though he may have practically ignored the Oxford Movement, Trollope's High and Dry attitude enabled him to do for us something of more importance: he contributes to our appreciation of the age as a whole. He preserves at its best the spirit of the 'fifties and the early 'sixties, when even Paget and Kingsley grew mild. It was in this period that the true Victorian Age bore its most characteristic fruit. And what flavor is at once so mild and yet so unmistakable? Humorous, romantic realism; kindly but penetrating criticism of social and individual faults; common sense; pleasant domesticity; a love of balance and permanence that to our own hectic age is as strange and restful as the incredible insularity, or even parochialism, of the circles in which life moved. Has the imagination ever conceived a civilization so quiet as that presented in the novels of this prosperous interlude?—the village with its old church, or the squire's manor and his neatly cultivated park, resting under the calm of an order where few assumptions are questioned, few values endangered. To get a true conception of Mid-Victorian England, one must mix many elements: Kingsley's typical compromise of naturalism with historical Christianity, the young-ladyism of Charlotte Yonge, the widespread reliance on law, custom, and normal feeling, suspicious of any too radical use of the intellect. There is a touch of all these qualities in the world of Trollope. And this period, to express itself adequately, developed the novel into an uncontroversial picture of manners moving with marvellous ease. Of this novel Trollope was a master unsurpassed. Though his picture of the clergy, because of its omissions, may not seem quite up-to-date, his novels in tone, method, and atmosphere, are superbly representative of the 'fifties and early 'sixties. In them is the sweet of Mid-Victorian peace, that old provincial genteel peace that still haunts the cathedral closes of England. It is as if Trollope, in spite of his ignorance of cathedral towns and of their more religious inhabitants, had been drawn to them instinctively as the setting artistically most suitable to the Mid-Victorian spirit, a home where it could linger on into another century.

PART III. THE RISE OF RITUALISM

CHAPTER XIII

TRANSITION: ESTHETIC AND SOCIAL

THE age which had opened with the Reform Bill of 1832 came to an end gradually between 1865 and 1880. With the death of Palmerton in 1865 there opened the Second Reform Era, marked by the extension of suffrage to the laboring class of the towns (in 1867) and by the Tests Act of 1871, which took from the Church of England her monopoly over the advantages of Oxford and Cambridge. England was becoming a modern democracy. The complacency of the Mid-Victorian period rapidly melted away. An agricultural depression began in the 'seventies. The power of the rural aristocracy was broken. Prosperity evaporated. Trade Unions grew in strength. Darwin's *Origin of Species* (1859) threw religion, already defending itself against geology and Biblical criticism, into perhaps the worst fright that religion has ever known. Swinburne's *Poems and Ballads* in 1866 were sensuously pagan, and, by the standards of the dying era, scandalous. The next half-century was marked by violent opposites: mystics and materialists (both going far enough away from the center to shock a Mid-Victorian), socialists and Neo-Catholics, esthetes and empire-builders, pessimists and utopians, rebels against form and poets who believed that form was everything. It was a period hard to characterize, because its various elements seemed to have little in common. But this similarity united most of the various schools: they recommended extremes, they breathed a spirit of rebellion. And they were in various ways sensational, according to different meanings of the word. The materialistic movement rested its philosophy on the validity of sensation as a test for truth. The novels adopted sensational plots. The Anglo-Catholics made a greater appeal to the senses through ritual. And the Neo-Romantics seemed downright sensual after the decorous 'fifties and early 'sixties. More than a word binds these movements together— they all denied the overlordship of calm Reason. Rebels and extremists united in ignoring balance or compromise.

In many ways the old atmosphere was being dissipated. England's mind expanded. She began to think more of the poor (who now enter literature less clownishly), more of that knowledge which had been called forbidden, more of her Empire. On the first day of the year 1877, Disraeli had Victoria proclaimed Empress of India. Abroad, Italy and Germany were shaped into nations, almost within the 'sixties. English interest in the rest of Europe grew. About this time, one may notice in the novels more mention of travel on the Continent.[1]

In other words, the Era was beginning which, in 1930, we were still calling our own. And not only in social setting, political outlook, and intellectual life was a transformation in progress. As to fiction, Hugh Walpole says that the 'seventies "cover the most markedly transitional period of the English novel, and they show so curious a meeting of opposite waters, so violent a contrast of men, methods, ideas and morals that there has been no other confusion quite so great in all the his-

---

[1] Mrs. Edwards, in *Creeds* (1859), actually portrayed with approval an Englishman educated in Germany, who when on the Continent abjured good English society and associated with peasants and struggling artists. International politics plays a large part in Henry Kingsley's *Silcote of Silcotes* (1867).

tory of English Letters."[2] Likewise, within the Anglo-Catholic Movement itself, there was a change, the most important that has occurred in the century since it arose at Oxford,—distinct enough to require a new word and to divide old leaders from new, namely, the rise of "Ritualism." Whether we think of the national (and even European) background, or of the novel as a form, or of the particular current of thought and feeling that is our subject, we find the "misty mid region" of the 'seventies a place where the old roads may no longer be followed. I wish to indicate enough of the tendencies during the transition to bring the period I have just dealt with to a close. To see how the Early-and-Mid-Victorian epoch ended, we must look at the boundary, which is anything but a pencil line.

The Ritualists were the second generation of the Oxford Movement, and they differed from the older Tractarians in being more democratic, more interested in proselyting, and (as their name implies) more concerned with ceremonial. The Tractarians had concentrated most of their attention on doctrine, personal culture, and the defense of existing institutions. The Ritualists were eager to mix with the people and win new kingdoms for the Church. They made more use of appeal to the senses, and they also exhibited a fervor that was much nearer to mysticism than the rather dry dogmatism of the Tractarians had been. Nor was the Ritualist so much of an enemy to the spirit of his own age as the Anglo-Catholic of the 'forties. The mysticism, estheticism, and symbolism of the end of the nineteenth century provided him with a congenial cultural atmosphere. Perhaps it would not be too much to say that the Tractarians seemed to concentrate on arresting changes, the Ritualists on furthering them.

[2] *The Eighteen-Seventies (Essays by Fellows of the Royal Society of Literature)*, 22.

The Ritualistic movement took place against a social background for the participants far different from that which the Tractarians had met with in the 'forties. Even the new extremists were not considered "un-English" as were their milder predecessors. The Anglo-Catholic was at last,—so many novels tacitly imply,—a recognized element in English life, not a foreign particle.[3] A new thrust could now take place without creating a panic. There had been an increase of tolerance on both sides throughout the 'fifties. I have already mentioned this development with regard to Paget and Kingsley, and it is also revealed by the fact that novels of manners displaced controversy. In 1859, in the preface to the fourth edition of *Yeast*, Kingsley himself says, "The Anglican movement, when it dies out, will leave behind at least a legacy of grand old authors disinterred, of art, of music; of churches too, schools, cottages, and charitable institutions, which will form so many centres of future civilisation. . . . I have said that Neo-Anglicanism has proved a failure, as seventeenth century Anglicanism did. . . ."[4] (This was written just before the rise of Ritualism.) On the other side, Charlotte Yonge, in the 1872 edition of *Abbeychurch*, which had satirized the Mechanics' Institute, says, "The wheels of this world go so quickly round, that I have lived to see that it would have been wiser in the clergyman to have directed rather than obstructed the so-called 'march of intellect.' " (Contrast her part in the crusade against intellect in the earlier period.)

Silcote of Silcotes (1867) by Henry Kingsley, brother of Charles, is one of the novels of the new age in which the Anglo-

---

[3] The Puseyite clergyman "belongs" not only in the novels of Yonge, but also in those of Trollope. Other examples: *The Young Curate, or The Quicksands of Life* (anon. 1857); Linton, *Lizzie Lorton of Greyrigg* (1866).

[4] Pp. ix-x.

Catholics appear as incidental figures, merely portrayed, not
attacked or defended. The clergyman, Algernon Silcote, im-
prudently "had declared for ritualism, and the pews would all
of them be empty in three months." His bills are therefore likely to be in arrears for some time.[5] He does not take the advice
of his father-in-law, Betts, who is indeed willing "to go into
the *moderately* High Church business; it is the paying one
. . ."[6] (Imagine saying that twenty years before! Truly, "Les
idées ont marché depuis 1845.'"[7]) Betts has pointed out to Algernon "that his church was not adapted for" High forms,
"being what you may call of an orthodox style of architecture"
and that the thing has never been made to pay commercially.
But Algernon will not listen. Nor will he even take time. "He
preached in his surplice the first Sunday I was away . . . he
turns the chairs towards the alter, and he calls that letting 'em
down easy." He empties his church, and is "prosecuted by his
churchwardens for lighting seven candles on his communion-
table before dark." But, says Betts, "what is orthodoxy in a
cathedral is Puseyism in a church. Architecture has a deal to
do with it; and we are going in for the highest style of architecture procurable for money."[8] The author treats Algernon
sympathetically. And one of the finest characters in the novel
is a member of a Sisterhood. Kingsley, with delightful irony,
makes Miss Heathton speak of the path by which a Protestant
girl may go astray: Arthur Silcote (High Church) first introduced Miss Lee to higher things, "to history, not merely

[5] XXII, 110.
[6] XXVI, 136. (The italics are mine).
[7] As Thureau-Dangin (*op. cit.*, III, 50) says, in contrasting what was
done to Ward for his *Ideal of a Christian Church* (1845) with the fact
that no one seriously thought of putting Pusey under the ban of the
church for his *Eirenicon* in 1865.
[8] XXVI, 139-143.

secular, but, I regret to say, ecclesiastical. He improved her wretched music, and in doing that took her away from her legitimate sphere at the piano, taught her the harmonium, and introduced her to such dangerous pieces as 'Stabat Mater.' He also incited her to church needlework and church decorations." Now the "poor girl thinks that, by accepting tradition, she can relieve herself of the responsibility of thinking for herself; that she can, by placing her conscience in the hands of a half-educated priest, bury the talent of intellect and free thought and free will with which God has largely gifted her."[9] Even in this novel, some bitter things are said of the Roman Church. "But the Jesuits promised her [the Princess] great things; and the Jesuits are good paymasters. They give what they promise. They give peace to fools."[10] The difference between the attitude towards Anglo-Catholic and Roman Catholic is striking.

Against this background we may define the main developments which differentiated Ritualism from Tractarianism. Among Anglo-Catholic novelists, the very earliest hints of a specifically *esthetic* emphasis we seem to owe more to Cambridge than to Oxford. One of the leading Puseyites produced by Cambridge, John Mason Neale (who subtracted Protestantism from *Pilgrim's Progress*)[11] in a letter dated Candlemas, 1844, said, "It is clear to me that the Tract writers missed one great principle, namely, the influence of aesthetics. . . ."[12] Neale was, while yet an undergraduate, one of the founders of the Cambridge Camden Society (1839) whose

[9] XXXIV, 182-183.
[10] XXXIX.
[11] See below, Appendix.
[12] Towle, *John Mason Neale,* 51. But even in his *Theodora Phranza* (1857) though this deals with the fall of Constantinople, there is little about ritual.

purpose was to study ecclesiology. That this was one of the earliest esthetic interests of the Tractarians, we can see from the large place church restoration held in the novels of the 'forties. Miss Sewell speaks of the rage for church building in 1844.[13] In Disraeli's *Sybil* (1845), " 'If this movement in the church had only revived a taste for Christian architecture,' said Lady Maud, 'it would not have been barren, and it has done so much more !' "[14] It was an Honorary Secretary to the Cambridge Camden Society, F. A. Paley, who wrote *The Church Restorers: A Tale treating of Ancient and Modern Architecture and Church Decorations* (1844),[15] the history of one church building since Saxon times. The author's spokesman in the portion dealing with contemporary conditions, says that an architect who wishes to erect a new pulpit and new pews "does not delight in architecture as a churchman," and "I assign the acknowledged inferiority of modern architecture (to speak generally) to three principal causes: the depraved taste of the day; the exclusively secular character of the science; and the want of *heart,* that is, energy and enthusiasm, in the generality of its professors." For a full comprehension of the spirit of Gothic architecture is required a religious view of the science and a sincere admiration for its ancient professors—not a contempt for their Faith.[16] Indeed, the speaker does not care for old churches merely because they are old, and contain beautiful things, but because he is "deeply interested in the noble works of the great days of the Church." He traces in the work fervent faith, and feels that attachment to the Church and respect for her ordinances are incalculably

[13] *Autobiography,* 80.
[14] I, II, xi, 240.
[15] Already mentioned, for its method, above, Ch. II.
[16] X, 113-116.

increased by the revival of care for her edifices.[17] So, even of one of the earliest Tractarians to write a tale advocating a greater attention to beauty, we cannot say that his interest in Catholicism arose out of conscious esthetic discontent, but rather the reverse. Obedience to Church authority was the first concern. In this tale, the Squire's wife says it is the worship of the heart, not of the eye, that we want, and though the rector answers that "The mind *must* be acted on by the senses . . . Religion *must* be aesthetic," he is "no advocate . . . for the captivating splendours of the Romish Church."[18]

In other words, even where we find what seem to be Tractarian roots of the Ritualistic Movement (narrowly considered), we still see that the latter was something of a minor revolution in worship. Ritualism was quite ready to make use of captivating splendours, and it turned to many arts besides architecture for means of appealing to the senses.

By the mid-'sixties,[19] the Oxford Movement had definitely gone beyond its early leaders. Pusey declared that he had never been a Ritualist, and said (in a speech before the English Church Union in 1866), "We had a further distinct fear with regard to ritual; and we privately discouraged it, lest the whole movement should become superficial."[20] Keble (according to Pusey, in 1851) never wore vestments, nor adopted "advanced ritual usages."[21] Newman, while some of his prac-

---

[17] IX, 83-87.

[18] XI, 127-128.

[19] See letter to Copeland (April 7, 1866), *Life and Letters of Dean Church*, 207 (meeting of old Tractarians and new Ritualists) ; Liddon, *Life of Pusey*, IV, 271f. Thureau-Dangin, *op. cit.*, III, 310f, 349f; Knox, *Catholic Movement in the Church of England*, 215f.

[20] Liddon, *Life of Pusey*, IV, 212.

[21] Storr, *Development of English Theology in the Nineteenth Century*, 267-268.

tices foreshadowed this later form of the Movement, was also suspicious of its more esthetic tendencies.[22]

The distinction is brought out clearly in some of the novels of the period. One of these says of a rector: "His theological views were those of the Keble and Pusey school. What are called 'High Church principles' were, at the time of Eustace Aylmer's ordination, well developed and pretty widely spread; but *Ritualism,* as we know it now, was in its very feeblest infancy . . ."[23] Gresley's *Bernard Leslie* already showed a shift of interest from dogma in the first part (1842) to ritual in the second (1859).

Charlotte Yonge's *The Three Brides* (1876) portrays three forms of Anglicanism: mildly High, mildly Low, and mildly secular. The Evangelical bride, Anne, does not think her husband's High Church brother is a Christian, for he bears all the tokens by which she has been taught to know a Papist.[24] She finally sees that her Puritan views were wrong. Secularity is here treated with least favor, and severely punished. As to High Churchmanship itself, Miss Yonge, a disciple of Keble, the Tractarian, issues a warning to extremists, *via* the (High) rector who says of two girls that "They are, if you understand me, technically reverent; they have startled the whole place with their curtsies and crossings in church; but they gabble up to the very porch; and the familiarity with which they discuss High Mass, as they are pleased to call it! I was obliged to silence them. . . ."[25] This is very clearly Mid-Victorian culture, with all its reserve, reprimanding a later taste. In Yonge's *The Pillars of the House; or Under Wode under Rode* (1873),

[22] Thureau-Dangin, *op. cit.,* III, 316.
[23] Worboise, *Overdale* (1869), II, 17; cf. also Ch. XII.
[24] I, xii, 185.
[25] II, i, 29, 30.

though "A great rubrical war had been fought out" at Bex-
ley, and the beauty of the restored church and the exquisite
services were much talked of, the congregations were thin and
the people indifferent, for the new Ritualist rector's sermons
lacked soul.[26] In this novel, Angela Underwood finds little comfort in the High Church system in which she has been bred.
She says of Ritualism that she has learned to rate "this frip-
pery" at its worth. She ceases to wear a cross. One clergyman suggests (with her brother, a High Church vicar, agree-
ing), that "her musical taste found ritual so congenial, that
excitability passed for devotion, in spite of the lack of trust-
worthy fruit of submission or selfdiscipline. . . ."[27] So she was
allowed to trust in the shell, in mere form. (Observe how the
point of this passage rests on the earlier assumption that a religion should be judged not, indeed, for its compatability with
fine taste but for its power to inculcate submission. It seems as
if Beauty had even been under suspicion exactly because it was
attractive.) At last we are told that Angela will probably soon
be allowed to become a candidate for membership in a religious
order.[28] In *Hopes and Fears* (1860), by Miss Yonge, which
I have already mentioned,[29] there are other warnings against
extremes. When Robert removes the little luxuries which have
been bought by others for his room, Honor Charlecote, "who
had lived long enough to be afraid of asceticism," says that he
is self-pleasing. His fellows will use "such conveniences of life
as come to them naturally." "Wilful doing right seldom tends
to good, above all when it begins by exaggeration of duty."[30]
Here submission, to whatever is, has been glorified even above

[26] I, i.
[27] IV, xliii, 235.
[28] IV, xlix.
[29] Above, Ch. X.
[30] I, x, 363.

"wilful" doing right. A Tractarian principle is being opposed to one which is at least Catholic. An attack upon the younger Anglo-Catholic priests is probably intended when Yonge says that it is one of Robert's remaining unwholesome symptoms that he rather enjoys persecution.[31] Obviously, if obedience to the authority set over us is the chief duty of man, martyrs are not only troublesome but wicked. The Ritualists did not think so, and were willing to go to jail rather than obey the law in conducting the church service.

Writers hostile to everything Anglo-Catholic likewise bear witness to the strong emphasis upon beauty among the Ritualists. In *Cousin Mabel's Experience of Ritualism* (1867), by Miss Whately, Cousin Mabel returns from abroad and finds three girls illuminating, embroidering, and painting glass for church decoration. Mabel thinks Titian's "Assumption of the Holy Virgin" a peculiar thing to copy for Protestant church-windows—the subject is "so utterly absurd and unscriptural."[32] We are likely to believe we are pleasing God with expensive church decoration when we are only gratifying our own taste; and it cripples our means of doing good to the poor, or of helping schools.[33] In *Undeceived; Roman or Anglican? a story of English Ritualism* (1877),[34] a dissenter says that popular religion today appeals chiefly to the esthetic. Religion offers a beautiful mystical symbolism; ceremonies "are all calculated to produce an evanescent sentimental feeling which people are only too apt to mistake for religion."[35] In *Overdale* (1869),[36] Lady Caroline says:

[31] I, x, 392.
[32] I, 7.
[33] I, 18-19.
[34] By Ruth Elliott (pseudonym for Lillie Peck).
[35] XVI, 156.
[36] By Worboise. See following chapter.

I do not think the *eclat* of going over to Rome is at all in good taste; but I assure you it is quite *ton* now to be *very high!* In the best circles there is just a certain clique that is Low Church, but the people who compose it are nobodies . . . one may as well be a Methodist or a Plymouth Brother as one of those dreadful, vulgar-minded Evangelicals! Eustace ought to be "high"; it is due to his rank that he should be so. It is the natural development of his aesthetic tastes and his Oxford training. . . .[37]

Meanwhile, there arose, with the new emphasis on cere-monial, a new social attitude that was almost as important. The Ritualists took up a more democratic position. This shift in the Anglo-Catholic Movement corresponds to that in the Tory party which appeared in the extension of suffrage to the lower classes in 1867, under the leadership of Disraeli. The parallel is close and important, since we have shown that the New Tories, and especially, Disraeli, began as the political counterpart of the Oxford Movement. An alliance with the rising proletariat might strengthen tremendously the side of re-ligion in the great war against unbelief, and defend the Church and Aristocracy from the liberal middle classes. In social as well as religious aspect, the Oxford Movement as a whole has often been confused with its Ritualistic phase, though the lat-ter did not begin until the second generation of the Move-ment. I have shown that the rank and file during the first gen-eration of the Movement did not seem to be motivated by, and that the leaders were often fighting against, those esthetic yearnings usually ascribed to them by opponents.[38] I have also supplied sufficient evidence to indicate that the Tractarians, in

[37] XIV, 131.

[38] Keble warned Charlotte Yonge against loving the Sacraments "for the sake merely of their beauty and poetry." Romanes, *Charlotte Mary Yonge*, 12.

their novels, instead of portraying the Upper Class coming to
the aid of the oppressed in opposition to intolerable business
men, were much more ready to preach that the poor should
reverence the rich, or to advocate Anglo-Catholicism as the
only thing which would make the wretches, for fear of God,
shun strikes and Mechanics' Institutes. If we had to depend
on our imagination for a picture of the early Oxford Movement, we might be pardoned for constructing it to suit our own
purposes, but with the books before us, we cannot ignore the
fact that the attitude of the Tractarians towards the populace
is represented by themselves as being less often one of pity than
of fear and contempt. At best, concern for the poor seldom
rose above the concern of a farmer for his oxen. But this
side of the case must not be overstated, even to balance previous misrepresentation. I have pointed out that there were seeds
of social radicalism in the Oxford Movement from the very
beginning; and tender-hearted women, with nothing else to do,
had patronized their inferiors generously whether encouraged
by High doctrine or Low. Disraeli, in *Sybil*, has one of his
noblest characters, planning a workingman's revolution, say,
"if we could only have the Church on our side, as in the good
old days, we would soon put an end to the demon tyranny of
Capital."[39] But Disraeli had a dangerously nimble wit. There
is, however, a witness from the opposite camp to say that the
seed was growing. In Kingsley's *Alton Locke* is mentioned a
a lord whose weak side is "a sort of High-Church radicalism."[40]
And when Alton says that in Christ's time Christianity was on
the side of the poor, his High Church cousin says he will mark
that card and play it when he gets an opportunity. "It may be

[39] III, VI, viii, 102.
[40] II, xxiv, 82.

a winning one in these democratic days."[41] And, by 1857, Kingsley has written this about a High Church curate:

> Frank was a gentleman and a Christian, if ever one there was. Delicate in person, all but consumptive; graceful and refined in all his works and ways; a scholar, elegant rather than deep, yet a scholar still; full of all love for painting, architecture, and poetry, he had come down to bury himself in this remote curacy, in the honest desire of doing good. He had been a curate in a fashionable London Church; but finding the atmosphere thereof not over wholesome to his soul, he had had the courage to throw off St. Nepomuc's, its brotherhoods, sisterhoods, and all its gorgeous and highly-organized appliances for enabling five thousand rich to take tolerable care of five hundred poor; and had fled from 'the holy virgins' (as certain old ladies, who do twice their work with half their noise, call them) into the wilderness of Bethnal Green. But six months' gallant work there, with gallant men (for there are High Churchmen there who are an honour to England), brought him to death's door. The doctors commanded some soft western air. Frank, as chivalrous as a knight-errant of old, would fain have died at his post, but his mother interfered. . . .[42]

In Henry Kingsley's *Stretton* (1869), the Puseyites are accredited with doing no end of good in civilizing London.[43] And a lord in a Radical speech demonstrates that Christianity and democracy are identical, and the only true formulas of Christianity are in the traditions of the Church, hence the only true democracy would be found in the formulas of the High Church party.[44]

Praise wrung from a hostile novelist is of a great deal more weight than mere claims of a partisan. In Mrs. Linton's *Lizzie Lorton of Greyrigg* (1866), the High Church rector's idea

[41] II, xxiv, 80.
[42] *Two Years Ago,* I, ii, 64.
[43] I, xiii.
[44] I, xviii, 270.

of Christian life includes absolute equality of social bearing with absolute spiritual supremacy.[45] And he thinks that the best thing to do with class distinctions is to abolish the need of them by refining the manners of the rougher element through kindly intercourse with the better educated. Margaret Elcome is of the same belief, and is endeavoring "to establish a kind of Christian socialism on a High Church basis. . . ."[46] In Mrs. Linton's *Joshua Davidson* (1872),[47] the hero, a carpenter, who associates with a Magdalene, finds in London an immense gulf between the Church and the workmen. "The parish priest, save in some chiefly ritualistic exceptions, scarcely exists."[48] Joshua is attracted by "the self-sacrificing lives of so many of the Ritualist party" but "fascinated as he was with the earnestness and culture of the Superior and his colleagues, they failed to hold him mainly because of the largeness of their assertions, the smallness of their proofs . . . their devotion to the Church rather than to Christianity at large," their ignoring of Christ's lowly birth, and similar factors. Their elaborate system of symbolism seems puerile, their central creed of sacrifice in the Eucharist, backed by their assumption of a priesthood possessing mysterious powers, fails to convince him. He tells the priest that *his heart has been captivated* and *his tastes charmed,* but his reason is not mastered.[49] Even in *Under Which Lord?* (1879), Mrs. Linton, though she attacks Ritualism viciously, does not attempt to deny that it is charitable to the poor. But the way she puts it is this: The vicar Lascelles tries "to break

[45] I, iv, 96. Linton will be discussed in greater detail in the following chapter. First, however, I have wished to borrow these remarks from her to illustrate the social attitude ascribed now to the Oxford Movement.

[46] II, vii, 200.

[47] I.e., a nineteenth-century Jesus, Son of David.

[48] IV, 62.

[49] IV, 64-67. (The italics are mine.)

down mental independence and manly self-respect" in the people, and "render habits of thrift" unnecessary by doles. "The vicar set great store by this charitable bribery which to him represented righteousness, and put out his strength to effect the personal and economic demoralization of men by means of this lavish almsgiving which is so powerful an agent in the hands of a proselytizing priest." Pauperism increases.[50] (It will be noticed that, in these three novels, though Mrs. Linton grows progressively more and more hostile to the Ritualists, she continues to bear witness to their care for the poor.)

A young High Church curate, Wentworth, is the hero of *The Perpetual Curate* (1864) by Margaret Oliphant. In Carlingford the slums were unknown to the minister of Salem Chapel, and to the late rector; they were known only to a half-dozen of the very élite and to the curate, "who was regarded by many sober-minded persons with suspicion as a dilettante Anglican, given over to floral ornaments and ecclesiastical upholstery. . . ."[51] Ultimately, Wentworth triumphs and becomes rector. The smug are evidently beginning to be shocked by Anglo-Catholics. Miss Dora, who is not High Church, is talking to her nephew, the curate:

> "but still I have a feeling that a clergyman should always take care to be respectable. Not that he should neglect the wicked," continued the poor aunt, apologetically, "for a poor sinner turning from the evil of his ways is the—the most interesting—sight in the world, even to the angels, you know; but to *live* with them in the same house, my dear—I am sure that is what I never could advise, nor Leonora either. . . ."[52]

A not uncommon figure in the novels of this period is the member of an Anglican Sisterhood. In Lady Georgiana Ful-

[50] II, viii, 177-178; 182.
[51] II, 8-10.
[52] VIII, 62-63.

lerton's *Mrs. Gerald's Niece* (1869), Edgar takes his wife, Ita, to a house of charity where an Anglican Sisterhood is carrying on works for the benefit of the poor. He thinks she will be favorably impressed by the Catholic appearance of this convent. But now that she has lost all belief in the Catholicism of the Church of England, though she admires the good works of the nuns, "there was something artificial and unreal in their studied imitation of the religious life, which she thought repulsive. The expressions in use among the so-called Anglo-Catholics grated on her ear. At that time, Mass, Benediction, Confession, were words which even in Sisterhoods were not in use. The bold innovations of the present day were not thought of, but there was an advance in that direction—the Puseyites were feeling their way, and approaching to the point the Ritualists have now reached. They . . . called Roman practices by Anglican names. . . ."[53] It will be noticed that, though the novel in which this Sisterhood appears was written in Ritualistic times, it refers to the Tractarian period. The same is true of Disraeli's *Endymion* (1880), where he says of Nigel Penruddock (who represents Manning, still in the English Church): "His church was always open, yet his schools were never neglected; there was a perfect choir, a staff of disciplined curates, young and ascetic, while sacred sisters, some of patrician blood, fearless and prepared for martyrdom, were gliding about all the back slums of his ferocious neighborhood. How came the Whigs to give such a church to such a person?"[54] It should be observed with regard to this last picture that, where it is a question of emphasis rather than of fact, a novel not avowedly historical usually gives a better idea of the interests of the time in which it is written than of the time in

[53] III, II, xii, 118-120.
[54] II, xxi, 206.

which the story is ostensibly laid. This is particularly true of *Endymion*.[55] Other novels in which a member of an Anglican Sisterhood appears are Henry Kingsley's *Silcote of Silcotes* (1867), Charlotte Yonge's *The Trial* (1864) and Eliza Lynn Linton's *Under Which Lord?* (1879).

We have shown in this chapter that by the time of the transition period which brought to a close the Mid-Victorian age, the Anglo-Catholic seems to have been looked upon no longer as either a devil or an apostle. He was recognized as a human being, and, moreover, an Englishman. And, whereas in the 'forties, the Oxford Movement had consciously opposed almost every current in contemporary thought and society, during the 'sixties and 'seventies it was moving in the same direction as some of the main streams of English culture: symbolism, estheticism, concern for the masses. The novels indicate that in the attitudes adopted by or towards the new phase of Anglo-Catholicism there was sufficient change to mark a turning point, but that each new attitude had sources in the Tractarian period. In the following chapters, we shall see what the novel was doing with the Oxford Movement in the Ritualistic period as subject matter for literature. Since it has been necessary first to give a picture of the background, a few details have already been drawn from some of the novels that are yet to be described.

[55] Another excellent example from this novel is the conversation on the symbolic meaning of the tournament (II, xxiii, 232). It belongs better to 1880 than to 1839, when the tournament upon which this was modelled took place.

CHAPTER XIV

THE NEW SENSATIONALISM

IN THE fiction that reflects the Oxford Movement in the 'sixties and 'seventies, we have a continuation of the development that had been in progress through the two preceding decades: there is more and more emphasis on the story *per se,* on the literary pleasures of plot, independent of ulterior purpose. (If propaganda had been superseded by moralizing Poetic Justice, the latter now fell before the claims of realism.) There is more emphasis on character, and this means a still farther concentration of focus; if the novels of the 'forties were concerned with national problems, and those of the 'fifties with the social life of domestic circles, the novelists of the transition were becoming interested chiefly in the subjective life of the individual. In some ways the method of this fiction seems to slip back—it again becomes sensational, and again we have discussion of religious doctrine. But in reality the Victorian novel no more returned upon its tracks than did the Elizabethan drama, however the slopes of decline may resemble the slopes of approach in lying considerably below the calm altitudes between. On both slopes, things are in motion—they do not rest perfectly on a center as they do at the apex. The sensationalism of the early novels was social and political, aimed at groups, capitalizing prejudice against Jesuit or Chartist or Socialist or Dissenter. Behind this was the implication that this or that will lead to revolution, or to institutional tyranny, or will save or ruin England. The sensationalism of the transition is within sight of the ivory tower, if it is not yet within it, for this is the sensationalism of passion and crime, that is, of individual life. What a wealth of material for literary treatment Anglo-Catholicism offered! The very dramatic themes of obedience to a spiritual director, or renunciation of the world for conventual life, these had in them enough possibilities to produce interesting fiction, even when the technical skill was small. A novelist setting out to show the effects of belief in celibacy of the clergy, in a world where the clergyman was often the most eligible matrimonial prospect in the community, had tapped a mine of excitement that would enrich even a mediocre talent. It is always hard to realize how men could have allowed such natural resources to lie in the ground year after year unexploited, though Mid-Victorian decency may have exercised a control too rigid to defy with profit. In 1859, Mrs. Edwards in *Creeds* shows a reaction against the genteel school (betraying in her account a not very accurate knowledge of the development of fiction, or of what qualities characterized different periods): Being old-fashioned, Estelle, when she read novels,

> actually sought for amusement therein (needless to say she read few English ones); she had a marked distaste for Blanche's favorite romances, written to further great principles—such as "Distortion," "Conversion" or "Dispensation,"—also those milder stories of the "Buttercups" school, which purport to set forth party-doctrines under the attractive garb of sacerdotal love-making, and are equally exciting in their delineation of both. She was uninterested by photographs of dull family existence, however correct. "The Inner Life of Mrs. Goody Two-shoes" was distasteful to her; the "Heart-agony" of elderly governesses simply repulsive. She acknowledged that she preferred men's writing to women's, save

when women wrote with the genius of George Sand or of Currer
Bell.[1]

The religious-discussion of the new period was no more
the same that we found in the 'forties than was the new sensationalism. The 'forties had emphasized theory, or, rather,
texts. The 'fifties had created characters interpreted in the
light of Anglo-Catholic doctrines. In the third period, the
characters themselves are concerned with living out Anglo-
Catholic ideas or opposing them. During the middle period,
the Oxford Movement had entered into the social life of England; in the third, it entered the mind. We even have a revival of controversy, but rather than serve as puppets or spokes-
men for the author the figures live an intellectual life of their
own and engage in controversy on their own behalf—the author retaining sometimes an esthetic objectivity so impartial
that we know he is not interested in furthering any program
but merely in studying the psychological implications of programs. Or if the author does enter the fight, he often has the
air of doing it because he sees, from scientific observation,
the evil effects on his characters of certain doctrines or practices; whereas in the earlier controversial period, the characters showed the evil effects because the author wished to fight.
The three stages are illustrated by the works, respectively,
of Paget, Miss Yonge, and Mrs. Linton. The difference between the novels of the 'forties and of the transition period
is also illustrated by a comparison of Disraeli's trilogy (dis-

[1] III, viii, 115. Yet the feminine realistic domestic novel of the inner life
of good women was to rise to greatness under George Eliot—and the heart-
agony of a governess had already been the theme of *Jane Eyre,* the greatest novel of "Currer Bell" (Charlotte Brontë). If a thing is old and yet
mediocre, we may safely scorn it; but it is never safe to scorn something
new, however unsuccessful it be as yet.

cussed in chapter IV), with his *Lothair* (1870) or his *Endymion* (1880). In these later works, Disraeli himself stays pretty well out of the battle. It is interesting to notice that in the middle period, less concerned with controversy, Disraeli wrote no novels. He was *not* a domestic novelist.

This detachment from the events that are being enacted in the novel is closely akin to estheticism. For the conception that a novel should not have a purpose but be merely a good story is almost Art for Art's sake in its most popular terms. Esthetic interest and concern for sense impressions appear in the fact that the novel develops from argument and exposition (in the period of the Tract writers) to a more extensive use of description and physical action (in the period of Ritualism). It is not contradictory to say that the development was from national to subjective problems, and also that it was from theory to sense-impression, for it is all part of one consistent change in interest from the general to the specific. Many causes may have contributed to this development. In the first place, it was natural to preach a faith abstractly when it was new, but to study individuals after the adherents of the faith had become familiar to the public. Again, the shock administered by "hard times" and "scientific" scepticism drove men to painful doubts and fears that increased their interest in the inner drama of the mind; and also encouraged them to take refuge in the esthetic delights which no philosophy can destroy. The earlier discontent could take on the aspect of class conflict and the defence of institutions, but it was hard to attribute Darwin to the French Revolution.

Unfortunately, the change from the Mid-Victorian to the following period was so much more gradual than that which occurred about 1850 that it is more difficult to define. And, of course, my summary refers only to general tendencies in those novels which take up the Oxford Movement. Probably many single pieces of fiction could be found in the 'sixties which would show few of the newer traits. I am speaking of fashions that rise and fall in chronological order, but this does not mean that one was buried before the other was born. The developments were noticeable enough for contemporaries to be conscious of them. Lady Georgiana Fullerton in *Mrs. Gerald's Niece* (1869) says that Christianity was never so violently attacked, but never less ignored.

> Whereas, some of the most popular authors of the beginning of this century could write volume upon volume of fiction with hardly a word in them indicatory that the thought of it ever crossed their minds; now scarcely a book of any sort is published which does not take sides. . . . While democracy rises . . . and men feel that, whether for good or for evil, the masses of their fellow-creatures must gain more and more power, the more eager . . . becomes the desire of the Christian and the Atheist, of the Catholic and the Infidel, to win them. . . . The immense change in England with regard to the books which take the greatest hold on the mind of youthful readers of the better sort, of those that shun in fiction unwholesome excitement, is strikingly exemplified when we contrast the works of Miss Edgeworth with those of Miss Sewell, those of Miss Austin [*sic*] with Miss Yonge's. Even Walter Scott's novels have almost ceased to charm the present generation. Stirring descriptions of historical events, glowing pictures of the pageantries of past ages, have far less interest, even for the young, than the analysis of character and revelations of a hidden life, which are often contained in the writings of the present day. Whatever treats of inward conflicts, secret perplexities, and the various trials of individual minds and hearts, necessarily commands attention. . . .[2]

At that time (1869), the writer could have found better examples of subjective novelists than Miss Yonge and Miss

[2] I, I, ii, 65-67.

Sewell, but in doing so she would have to admit the fiction of "unwholesome excitement." The "novel of ideas" and the "sensation novel" were not separate genres. Moreover, her choice of Miss Yonge and Miss Sewell for illustration supports my argument that the domestic novel, especially that dealing with Anglo-Catholicism, was a definite predecessor of the later works that studied so carefully the inner life. Our stages are all merely parts of a continuous development. *Mrs. Gerald's Niece* itself shows great progress beyond the same author's *Ellen Middleton* (1844), a rather silly melodrama. *Mrs. Gerald's Niece* shares particularly the objectivity of the new age. The arguments with which the writer disagrees are nevertheless presented in a spirit of fairness. Though she is Catholic, she portrays the Protestants favorably.

In 1868, Paget published *Lucretia; or the Heroine of the Nineteenth Century*, written as a satire on the sensational novels of the day. He says the principles of these novels are so demoralizing, "the conversations retailed so revolting for their looseness, wickedness, and blasphemy; the scenes represented so licentious, or so horrible" that it is the duty of anyone who can "to do what in him lies, to preserve the purity of the young, by putting them on their guard against the perusal of writings . . . which really seem directed to one purpose only; the perversion of our whole fictional literature, by a process as insidious as it is demoniacle,—that, namely of calling evil good, and good evil . . . with each new novel of that type being more 'exciting' from its profligacy, its moral depravity, and its irreligion. . . . But what remedy is there for the hearts they have already corrupted, and the purity they have destroyed? for the consciences they have darkened and deadened, for the souls which, through their instrumentality, have perished?"[3] I have said that at this period the lower classes be-

[3] 298-9.

gan to enter literature less clownishly. Paget manages to include them in his scorn:

> If such filthy Yahoos . . . [as the novels portray] . . . do really
> exist . . . there is at least this comfort, that, as yet, they keep in
> the background; they do not obtrude themselves on our notice;
> they are a race as strange to us as the Fuegians would be. . . . But
> strange they will not long continue, if the rage for sensational nov-
> els continues. . . . Already incalculable mischief has been done
> among the upper and middle classes, through their insatiate peru-
> sal, for years past, of all this pernicious nonsense. It is impossible
> not to observe many indications of a resolution in the rising gen-
> eration to cast off many of those restraints which the people called
> Christians have believed to be imposed upon them by the laws of
> GOD; to set all authority, parental, social, and political, at defi-
> ance;[4] [What the people called Christians believe politically ap-
> pears shortly.]
> Most of the worst sensational novels are republished, vile type
> and vile paper combining to secure for the dissemination of still
> viler sentiments a very low price. . . . A sensualized individual is,
> *pari passu,* a brutalized one; . . . If our humbler classes only read
> in order to be sensualized, there is only one possible result. France
> is not the only country in the annals of the world in which a reign
> of lust has been followed by a reign of terror.[5]

Through the teaching of these novelists, "murder has been
made easy to the meanest capacity . . . all breaches of the
seventh commandment are provided with apologetic excuses;
antenuptial connections are treated of as inevitable; adultery as
a social necessity."[6] Some of these writers are women "and
the worst of them, UNMARRIED WOMEN !"[7] (The emphasis is Paget's.) And he makes a plea for the older realism,
since the sensational events of real life are rare and, even when

[4] 300-301.
[5] 302.
[6] 303.
[7] 305.

they come, are commonly unromantic. "Our shins are more frequently broken by the coal-scuttle, than our hearts by disappointment in love."[8] There speaks the Mid-Victorian spirit in all its narrowness and some of its wisdom, prosaic and idealistic. Paget, by the way, was the one who, in *The Warden of Berkingholt,* had sugared Tractarian propaganda with a certain amount of crime.[9]

Let us examine somewhat in detail the novels which illustrate the narrative practices we have mentioned. In any form of Catholicism, of course, the element that lent itself best to sensational treatment was that of sex. This involved, on the one hand, celibacy, and on the other, what one of Henry Kingsley's characters calls "the pretensions of the priest to dictate in our domestic arrangements."[10] In *High Church* (1860), by Frederick William Robinson, a wife is so much attracted by the Anglo-Catholic zeal of the new clergyman that she goes to church even when her husband has asked her not to. This disturbs the happiness of their home. She pours forth in the confessional what should have been sacred "to God and her husband."[11] Though she is innocent, she gives her husband reason to be justly suspicious of her relations with the curate. Besides this jealousy, the introduction of High Church practices causes other dissension in the parish. Pamphlets appear teaching everything but peace on earth, good will amongst men, and the place is "at red heat, discussing theology."[12] But it is decoration, not doctrine, that makes the trouble. Visitors even come from adjacent villages to see the Anglo-Catholics. And the story is not one of argument, but of action. Be-

[8] 309.
[9] See above, Ch. II.
[10] *Silcote of Silcotes,* XXXIV, 181.
[11] I, II, v, 240.
[12] I, II, i.

sides conflicts between mob, clergy, and leading citizens, there is the murder of the curate, laid at the door of the jealous husband. Add that the author does not entirely condemn or justify any one party, and that he treats with sympathy a low character as if one of "the poor" could exist as a human being. It will be seen that this novel illustrates very well the new attitude of fiction.

Overdale; or, The Story of a Pervert (1869), by Emma Jane Worboise (whose *Amy Wilton* we discussed with the controversial tales of the 'forties) is built around the problem of celibacy, though confession and ritual are also important. An Anglican clergyman, who likes to call himself a priest, goes Higher and Higher until he gives up his wife and family and joins the Church of Rome. Later, after his wife's death, he sees his error and comes back to his children. Considerable space is devoted to portraying the control exercised by the clergyman over the women of the community—how he subdued saucy Kate Chennery, how Roberta Roberts would not submit to much restraint, how Agatha, falling in love with him, "felt a strange delight in doing his will, submitting herself even in thought to his smallest expression of judgment."[13] The Misses Harrison, having nothing else in particular to do, are High Church. They practise with the choir, go to church, and arrange garlands of flowers.[14] Another woman finds the system of piety which prevails at Overdale repulsive:

> Either you are to be mortifying the flesh and the affections, saying countless prayers in a damp church, and half-starving yourself on particular days, or else you are to be absorbed in some musty old canon, and in Church millinery, chasubles, albs, stoles, copes, and all the rest of the rubbish, and to work altar cloths, and

[13] XII, 111.
[14] XXVIII.

hassocks, and *prie-dieux*, and embroidered priestly robes! The whole life is unnatural, senseless.[15]

Rosamund Aylmer can kneel before a graven image and press it with her lips, but she dreads lest her affection for her brother should become "idolatry."[16] Her unrequited lover, Ralph Mornington, suggests that her absorption in devotional exercises may proceed from sublimation, or as he puts it, in that mild Victorian language which has led many to think that Freud discovered something new, "an intensity of sentiment, which lacks any natural object on which to expend itself." Consequently, she may listen to a proposal of matrimony.[17] Throughout, the authoress glorifies marriage as instituted by God.[18] The novel also boasts a Jesuit who "comes and goes like a shadow."[19] There is more description of setting and local color than was common in the novels of the earlier period. The real purpose seems to be not propaganda, but the telling of a story, and for that the author has an unusual amount of talent. Few of the very minor novels mentioned in this thesis hold the interest so well.

A more exciting psychological novel is Eliza Lynn Linton's *Under Which Lord?* (i.e. Should a wife obey husband or priest?), calculated to inspire a loathing towards Anglo-Catholicism. For us the most interesting thing about this novel of 1879 is that it uses a plot somewhat similar to that of Mrs. Trollope's *Vicar of Wrexhill* (1837). Money is unwisely left in the hands of a woman,—unwisely because she is easy prey for a clergyman. But in Mrs. Trollope the clergyman was Evangelical. Here he is Anglo-Catholic. Besides showing

[15] XXIX.
[16] XXVI.
[17] XXXV.
[18] E.g., XXXII, 309.
[19] XXIX, 270.

Catholic rather than Evangelical religious excitation as the force which will lead a woman astray, *Under Which Lord?*, true to the new sensationalism, makes the husband play an important part in the story. Richard Spence has married Hermione Fullerton, though she is wealthier than he. His life endeavour is to weaken the hold of Christianity on the minds of men "by substituting knowledge for superstition," for he believes "the influence of the Church the consolidation of intellectual darkness. . . ."[20] At first, the marriage is a success, but as he grows less demonstrative, though his affection is still as deep, she becomes unhappy, for she wants continual excitement. The new vicar, Launcelot Lascelles, is one of the most advanced of Ritualists, "assuming quasi-divine powers."[21] He "was a Roman Catholic in all save name and obedience, being his own pope and college of cardinals in one; absolute by right of ordination, and owing no submission to, the heads of the Church whereof he was an inferior member, nor to the laws of the country whereof he was a citizen, should either displease him—one who was contemptuous of modern science, sceptical of modern progress, and opposed to all forms of mental freedom."[22] Hermione gains, in religious enthusiasm, "a new love if you will, which the conscience approves and which neither the husband nor society can condemn. . . ."[23] Were Lascelles not a celibate clergyman, the profane world would have been justified in imagining that he was flirting with the wife of Richard Fullerton,[24] and she was soon "giving to another man than her husband the same unquestioning obedience" that she had him.[25] For "sex when most ignored is oftentimes most

[20] I, i, 14-15.
[21] I, ii, 27.
[22] I, ii.
[23] I, iii, 63-4.
[24] I, iv, 75. (Richard was required to take his wife's name on marrying.)
[25] I, iv, 90.

potent; and the priest is no less the man to his female devotees because he offers himself to them as a saint."[26] The clergyman points out that Hermione owes a higher duty to "God" than to her husband.[27] He says that she should spurn her anti-religious husband from her as a viper.[28] At last she is forced, on pain of excommunication, to take the management of her estate out of her husband's hands and refuse to let him continue his agnostic lectures, or rent cottages to his followers among the poor (who have been dispossessed). Lascelles gets her spiritually drunk. "She had no sense of morality, no conscience beyond obedience, and was in that state wherein women have . . . flung their darlings to the lions when commanded by the high priest, who to them was the voice of their god."[29] At last Lascelles gives up his belief in celibacy and marries another woman. Hermione, enraged because he has deserted his principles, goes back to her husband, who dies with his face irradiated with glory as he thinks of the victories over superstition, the spread of knowledge, the peace of nations, the unfettered progress of humanity which will come.[30] Let us notice others of what the author calls the vicar's "spiritual harem."[31] With "the spiritual philandering with which a celibate priesthood enforces dogmatic teaching,"[32] he wins over to Ritualism Theresa, a hysterical girl.[33] How handsome Mr. Lascelles looked!—"the very ideal of a well-born, well-bred High Priest." Theresa, "hysterical for want of sleep" and food, is faint with passionate ectasy,

[26] I, ix, 205-206.
[27] I, iv, 98.
[28] I, xi.
[29] III, vii, quotation, p. 173.
[30] III, xii.
[31] II, i, 3.
[32] III, i.
[33] I, vi.

and "her rapt look of personal adoration, startled Mr. Lascelles himself, used as he was to the passionate love of women disguised as religious fervour—to the personal adoration of so many before her, whom, like her, he had spiritually seduced for the good of the Church." But he thinks Theresa a good subject for vivisection.[34] At this time, "The vicar and the Almighty were getting sadly entangled" in the minds of Hermione and Theresa, "and to obey Mr. Lascelles was to both perilously synonymous with obeying God; which was exactly the state of mind that he wished to produce."[35] In confession Theresa finds it sweet to lay bare her secret soul and give Lascelles the greatest gift a woman can bestow, her spiritual freedom, her reserve. He presses her to him, kisses her forehead, and caresses her with his hand.[36] As she dies, the presence of priests, and extreme unction, "unwholesome excitement," disturb her peace. We have a death-bed scene to show how horrible it is to die a Christian. After reason and hope have fled, the terrors of death, the fears of Hell, remain.[37] Aunt Catherine Molyneux has also been won over to Ritualism, and her imagination awakened by a dream of heavenly espousals. She comes to the Harvest Festival dressed in white, which she means should express bridal array. Lascelles checks her by asserting Church control.[38] Over Virginia, the daughter of Richard and Hermione, the vicar exerts a power so horrible that she, "who never did anything useful in her life" (as another character puts it), now "cleans those large heavy candlesticks with plate-powder and wash-leather, just as our footman cleans the plate."[39] Ringrove says the natural pride and

[34] I, x, 225-226.
[35] I, xi, 237.
[36] I, xi.
[37] III, x.
[38] I, x, 228-229; I, xi.
[39] II, iii, 73.

respect of a girl is broken by putting her to degrading work.[40]
This passage by Mrs. Linton illuminates the meaning of the
statement at the end of *Overdale*,[41] that Ritualism is sapping
the foundations, not only of the Church, "but of our national
glory, and of our social and domestic joys and respectability."[42]
What Miss Yonge or Miss Sewell would have praised as obedience, Mrs. Linton in *Under Which Lord?* calls "superstitious
belief in the power of the priesthood—in the sinfulness of
reason—in the lost condition of the soul which dares to doubt
and hesitates to obey—."[43]

Under Which Lord? associates Ritualism with estheticism
and Medievalism. The Harvest Festival is described with its
elaborate ritual and decoration, "the lure" that should bring
the people to accept the Church's doctrines and decrees. The
men of the village thought this was "taking liberties with the
Constitution,"[44] admirable illustration of the conflict of esthetic
innovation with a rooted tradition. Cuthbert Molyneux, who
deliberately placed "emotion" and "realization" above reasoning, was a very woman in feeling the need for a director or
superior.[45] At Cambridge, he "had distinguished himself by his
romantic Ruskinism. . . .[46] "Cuthbert, already devoted to Bach
and blue china, reverencing Botticelli and despising Raffaele,
had yielded without difficulty to the new régime of aesthetic
piety and mediaeval affectation. . . ." (But Ringrove Hardis-
try, "practical rather than aesthetic, a citizen rather than a
sectarian, of the broadest section of the Broad Church" had

[40] II, iv, 97.
[41] By Worboise.
[42] LI, 496.
[43] III, v, 121.
[44] I, x, 224.
[45] I, vi, 138.
[46] I, iii, 64-65.

resisted.)[47] When a woman faints from weakness and feverish imagination induced by Catholic practices, Virginia . . . "prayed fervently to the Blessed Virgin as her contribution to the healing methods of the moment; and Cuthbert mechanically took up the thurible and swung a cloud of incense into the room."[48] Cuthbert also adopted a "somewhat quaint form of speech as sounding simple and antiquated," and he liked to sit in attitudes copied from Medieval pictures.[49]

In Linton, as in Worboise, argument is carried on, not by mere scholarly proof or doctrine *versus* doctrine, but by passionate discussion in dramatic situations. Yet even here the writer makes an attempt to state with impartiality the thoughts in the minds of the High Church characters, and she credits them with sincere devotion to a cause, a degree of tolerance not extended to the Protestant extremists by Mrs. Trollope in the *Vicar of Wrexhill* or by Sinclair Lewis in *Elmer Gantry*. And in *Lizzie Lorton of Greyrigg* (1866), though the novel belongs with the sensational school, Mrs. Linton makes an extremely High Church rector the noblest character in the book. But unfortunately she refers very little to his religion. We have already shown that *Lizzie Lorton* and *Under Which Lord?* both bear witness to the attitude towards the lower classes among the Ritualists.

Later, in Buchanan's *Foxglove Manor* (1884), we again have the under-which-lord triangle: a Ritualist clergyman of celibate ideals, popular with the women, a Ritualistic lady of the manor, and her agnostic husband engaged in scientific studies. This is a violently cheap novel, with a mysterious "bloodthirsty" Spaniard, elixir of death, and such claptrap.

[47] II, ii, 33-34.
[48] II, x, 254.
[49] II, x, 260-263.

Every character, every device, is crude and blatant. The vicar here actually seduces a girl, and then tries to break away from her while making love to another man's wife. Sensationalism even invaded the novels of Miss Yonge, for in *The Trial* (1864), as the title suggests, there is not indeed passion but crime—namely, murder.

Margaret Oliphant in *The Perpetual Curate* (1864),[50] even more than these other novelists, makes use of religious divisions merely for the psychological situations they produce. When a rector is thinking of going over to Rome, his wife, threatened with being put aside, sees *not* the slight difference between Rome and the highest Anglicanism, but life going to pieces.[51] The author is interested in religious problems and practices entirely as matter for story. Her tolerance goes so far that she treats with sympathy Evangelical, High Church, Romanist, and the old secular squire who says his idea of Church and State is: The eldest son, squire; the second, rector.[52] It is this squire who says, "As for the Church of Rome, it's Antichrist—why, every child in the village school could tell you that; and if Gerald entertains any such absurd ideas [to the contrary], the thing for him to do is to read up all that's been written on the subject, and get rid of his doubts as soon as possible."[53] This novel contains a mysterious stranger, who is a criminal and—sufficiently unorthodox juxtaposition—the brother of the girl with whom the curate is in love. But that is nothing compared to the fact that the curate is suspected of a seduction committed by the criminal.

Celibacy forms the theme of Charles Reade's *The Cloister and the Hearth. A Tale of the Middle Ages* (1861). This novel

[50] Its picture of social work has already been discussed.
[51] XV.
[52] XLI, 354.
[53] XVII, 127.

was begun periodically in *Once a Week* (1859) under the title
of "A Good Fight."[54] But because of a quarrel with the editor
Reade was asked to stop the novel in the same year.[55] He con-
cluded it suddenly with a premature ending. In this earlier version of the novel, the journey to Germany and Italy is sketched
in a few words. It would be hard to say how much of the story
was already in the author's mind when he ended "A Good
Fight" happily, with wedlock. But, in view of the trend just
about that time towards treatment of Catholicism with reference to sex, it is interesting to notice that this 1859 version does
not show the theme of cloister *versus* hearth. The difference
in title would imply that Reade had not yet conceived his story
as it now stands. Moreover, the chief references to Catholicism
are in those portions of *The Cloister and the Hearth* that did
not appear until 1861. These references are remarkably neutral.
While the reader is left with an adverse opinion of "poly-
theistic" adoration of the Virgin and the Saints,[56] and the
author even goes so far as to speak of the doctrine of the Im-
maculate Conception as a Pope's crotchet, he treats confession
favorably.[57] His sympathy for devotion to the Church is so
deep that the epithet "vile heresy"[58] applied, at the end, to the
celibacy of the clergy seems to be a note appended to make the
author's private attitude clear beyond a doubt. It is only occasionally that he seems to betray unconsciously a Protestant
attitude—for example, when Margaret shows Gerard that the
hermit leads a life of spiritual egotism. She calls him to the
"higher" life of doing battle in the world.[59]

[54] Vol. I, Jan. to June.
[55] Reade and Reade, *Charles Reade,* II.
[56] LV, 424-428; LXXII, 521-522.
[57] XCVI, 675; LXIX, 509.
[58] XCIX, 701.
[59] XCV, 662-664.

Reade's *Griffith Gaunt; or, Jealousy* (1866) is the story of a man who marries a Roman Catholic. She is attracted by a priest, though she is quite unconscious of any erotic element in her interest. But the priest is quite definitely in love with the wife. When she finds it out, she uses her influence to get him transferred away from her parish. The husband's jealousy makes the story. It even leads him to commit bigamy. If the novel did not fall so pat with its contemporaries in the treatment of the psychological possibilities of certain elements in the Catholic system, we should not have noticed it, for it is concerned with the Roman, not the Anglican Church. But we can see, by comparing it to the other novels of the 'sixties and 'seventies which we have just discussed, that even the eighteenth-century setting of the story has failed to remove it completely from current interests. The Catholic priest, though portrayed as a Romanist, is an exact counterpart of the Ritualistic clergy who figure in these other novels of contemporary life. He is a gentleman-saint, esthetic and fervent. He has sufficient artistic talent to draw Mrs. Gaunt's picture from memory.

Compton Reade tells us that Charles, in order to write *The Cloister and the Hearth* "had, perforce, to surmount a congenital distaste for all things mediaeval."[60] His success was remarkable, for few pieces of nineteenth-century literature have more gusto. Reade studied his material with an attitude almost scientific. In *Griffith Gaunt,* he says, "But a great fault once committed is often the first link in a chain of acts, that look like crimes, but are, strictly speaking, consequences."[61] Reade belongs with the novelists who were serious students of the results of moral decisions. In this, in his position of schol-

[60] Reade and Reade, *Charles Reade,* 88.
[61] III, ii, 30.

arly and esthetic detachment from the problems that agitate his characters (even when he had a definite bias or purpose), in his sensationalism, in his interest primarily in plot and passion, he was a great master of the kind of fiction that dealt with the Oxford Movement during the early days of Ritualism.

CHAPTER XV

JOSEPH HENRY SHORTHOUSE
QUAKER-CATHOLIC

BETWEEN 1866 and 1876, Joseph Henry Shorthouse wrote *John Inglesant,* not only the greatest Anglo-Catholic novel of the Victorian Age but, as Paul Elmer More judiciously calls it, the "nearest approach in English to a religious novel of universal significance."[1] This is a story of the religious quest, the search for the True Way of Life, laid in England and Italy in the seventeenth century and among some of the spiritual seekers of that profound and noble epoch. Materials from the writings of Hobbes, Ellwood, Burton, John Aubrey, are actually incorporated into Shorthouse's text, where they are so little out of place that few readers have noticed the borrowings.[2] The novel was not printed until 1880. By that time, the Mid-Victorian Age had closed. Moreover, the boundaries of the Oxford Movement were beginning to blur. Impact of new ideas, development of germs within, indeed the very harmony of Anglo-Catholicism with other currents of later nineteenth-century culture, and its own influence on the outside world, make it difficult to define the limits of the Movement. High Churchmen as early as 1889, in *Lux Mundi,* began to use rather than to oppose the work of science and

[1] *Shelburne Essays Third Series,* 236.

[2] For some of the more fascinating parallel passages, see W. K. Fleming, "Some Truths About 'John Inglesant,'" *Quarterly Review,* CCXLV, cdlxxxv, July, 1925.

scholarship. The religion of Shorthouse was described by a friend as "Broad Church Sacramentarianism."[3] One thinks of his tolerance, his lack of dogmatism, his heretical willingness to consider ideas on other grounds than that of Church authority. The author's complaint that "few have deduced English Churchmanship from my book,"[4] is a remarkable illustration of the breadth of his position. He was born in 1834, a Quaker, and did not join the English Church until 1861, only five years before he began *John Inglesant*. The specifically Tractarian Movement that had inspired Paget, Gresley, Heygate, the Sewells, Yonge and Skene was already moribund. Moreover, much of Shorthouse could be accounted for by his Platonism. Again I agree with Mr. More: "That Mr. Shorthouse was able to write a book which is in a way the direct fruit of" the Ritualistic "conflict, and still contains so much of the universal aspect of religion, came, I think, from his early Quaker training and from his Greek philosophy."[5] Yet, in spite of these other traditions, or perhaps with their assistance, in *John Inglesant* Anglo-Catholicism, as we know it today, was beginning to find itself. This, I believe, no critic-historian could deny.

The later novels by Shorthouse are of less importance to us, for themselves, but we may draw from them background to supplement our study of his masterpiece. *Sir Percival: A Story of the Past and the Present* (1886) casts over Victorian life a Medievalizing haze. The story is laid among old edifices, chivalric society, and forests. The chief modern element in the book is the agnosticism it brings in to refute. Soon after Constance Lisle (the narrator) meets Sir Percival, she recalls a

[3] Smith, J. H., "Introduction," *Life, Letters, and Literary Remains of J. H. Shorthouse* by his wife, I, p. xii.
[4] *Life, Letters . . . (etc.)*, 398-399. (Quoted by Miss J. D. Montgomery.)
[5] *Shelburne Essays Third Series*, 228.

sentence from Malory, and she silently prays that he may achieve a fame not dissimilar to that of his namesake.[6] (She frequently turns to Malory, even in describing the scenery.) Sir Percival dies in Africa, after having received the Sacrament by eating three blades of grass. When Constance receives a packet from the West Coast, into her mind flashes what she had read to Percival from the Morte d'Arthur, " 'And I saw a damoysel, all in white, with a vessel in both her hands.' " She says, "I felt that in some way, at present unknown to me, I held in my hands a sacred trust—a letter to be read nowhere but before the altar of the Lord."[7] The packet contains a Victoria Cross. Sir Percival has found the Holy Grail. Just exactly what the Holy Grail symbolizes would be hard to say,—Death, Purity, Christ, mystical union with God. It is the essence of this sort of symbolism to create vague suggestions.

The Countess Eve (1888) is even more symbolistic. It is a story of an Eve, wife of the Count du Pic-Adam, who almost commits adultery because of malefic influences, but is deterred, just as she is preparing to meet her lover, by this: "the moment that she passed the threshold, she saw It for the first time. It was only for a second. All the powers of Hell, all the glamour and delusion and sorcery at the command of the Prince of Evil, were exerted at the moment to recall the false step, to cancel the sight; but it was too late. She had seen, by the power and light of God's conscience in a pure spirit—she had seen, at the moment of a fatal error, the face of committed Sin. What she saw she never knew. The horror of the sight, whatever it was, blasted her memory, and left it so far a

[6] III.
[7] XI.

ghastly blank. She sank upon her knees before the still open door of Paradise . . ."[8] (her garden with a Tree of Life in it). How the power of hell, and the glamour, were exerted on her we are not told. Indeed, it is another characteristic of this symbolism not to require causes and motives for human reactions. We are not in the vulgar world of phenomena, but living with personified essences. The symbols of this story are a little confused—Eve does not seem to be thought of as one who might tempt her husband, and Satan takes at least two forms. Indeed, the reader cannot be very sure that it was adultery which Eve would have committed if she had not seen the blasting It, but that is what the story seems to shadow forth. At least, she was headed towards some very evil act.

Blanche, Lady Falaise (1891), tells of a woman who considers herself in love with a man because she thinks she sees in him the perfection she has ascribed to herself. He jilts her and marries wealth. Having committed such a sin, of course he takes to drink and other evil courses. Lady Blanche, whom he wronged, thinks that, because she is the victim, she has thus ruined him body and soul. She commits a "terrible, a nameless sin,"[9] that is, she tries to take on herself another person's sin and punishment. These two people who were not really in love with each other both ruin themselves with remorse because they did not get married. This is an example of the way people sometimes act and think in Shorthouse's novels. Here the moral problem is delicate indeed, but it is solved by a supernatural pronouncement. There is a vision of Lady Falaise, before an altar, and an unspeakable light that no man can approach unto, and words saying, "Thou hast tried to offer a

[8] IX, 202.
[9] II, iii, 236.

sacrifice which it was not for thee to offer, and to bear a punishment which was not thine to suffer or to bear. Nevertheless, the sacrifice which thou hadst to offer is accepted, and the punishment which was thine thou hast fully borne. Thy prayer is heard. His sins, which are many, are forgiven him."[10] Just then, the forgiven man enters the room, pale and worn, but with a new look on his face. If the early Anglo-Catholic novelists were incredibly prosaic, Shorthouse has almost made up for it by giving us stories where supernatural forces may appear at any moment.

Shorthouse described *John Inglesant* as "an attempt at a species of literature which I think has not hitherto had justice done to it . . . Philosophical Romance."[11] The same phrase would fit his other novels. In them the characters lead intellectual lives of their own. They are not puppets in the hands of an author for the illustration of his own opinions, though they themselves discuss ideas a great deal. Shorthouse retains an esthetic detachment so impartial that usually the arguments are brought to no conclusion. He seems to be curiously comparing various excellent ideas, and by subtle suggestion or by the turn of the plot allowing the reader himself to see which is superior. One of the instruments of Philosophical Romance is symbolism, the counterpart in art of Ritualism in the Church. Both are used to express spiritual conceptions which lie beyond the reach of human reason.

All of Shorthouse's fiction is a step beyond the other work we have examined in that it richly exemplifies the New Description—perhaps too richly. One of the features of the esthetic movement was the development of the art of prose

[10] II, v, 287.
[11] Preface to New Edition, 1881, *John Inglesant*, I, p. v.

description,—accompanied, or perhaps made possible, by an increase in the complexity of prose style. Description was used now not merely to indicate the setting but for its own beauty, or for purposes of symbolism, or to magnify the setting into one of the forces in the plot. In essay and romance, Ruskin, Pater, Hardy, Kipling, and Stevenson cannot be matched in this respect by Scott, Macaulay, Dickens, or Thackeray. Descriptive power, vague symbolic suggestion, and conscious style (a style calm and meditative in manner, but suggesting by its rhythm impending doom and suppressed feverish excitement) contribute to build up in *John Inglesant* an atmosphere of the supernatural that is hardly surpassed in any English novel. And Shorthouse's assumption that the supernatural is real beyond the shadow of a doubt also strengthens his ghostly fiction. In conveying this effect, he carries the subjective interest of fiction very far. He makes constant use of all sorts of premonitions. We might say that, artistically, he justifies the supernatural by employing an interpretation similar to that arrived at philosophically by William James in *The Varieties of Religious Experience,* that is, by turning to "the recesses of feeling, the darker, blinder strata of character." This is leagues away from the dogmatic clarity of the Tractarians. *John Inglesant* has the same theme found in so many of their novels: the religious quest, leading to Anglo-Catholicism. But the earliest novels made a concrete appeal to Church history and to Biblical texts, with good hard footnotes for support. Here it is an attempt to reach God mentally, to do right in the midst of fundamental doubts, the very entertainment of which would have been a sin to any of the Tractarian novelists.

Nevertheless, the "Philosophic Romance" as a form was not a new genre, but merely a new development. It does belong to the late Victorian period because of its emphasis on story, on subjective conflict, on description; and because of the author's detachment. But it had plenty of forerunners, in a line[12] running back to Paget and Gresley. In Shorthouse dialogue is very important, and some of the speeches are long expositions. We have not seen much of this type of fiction since we left the 'forties, and now it is done with more tolerance and a great deal wider appreciation of different points of view than was common before. In causation, Shorthouse is as independent of materialistic determinism as Newman; the Grace of God works wonders—for instance, the conversion of Malvolti. Coincidences are numerous.[13] Causes of events grow out of the spiritual nature of the universe, in which such a man as Inglesant would be led by God in a certain way.[14] Like his predecessors in the 'forties, Shorthouse depends for his characterization too much on the inadequate device of giving long extracts from a man's conversation—if, indeed, he thought at all about creating character. As in the 'forties, the *dramatis personæ* represent points of view. The four novels I have mentioned also resemble the earlier novels in that the love affairs do not end happily. But Inglesant does marry, and in this, more than in most Tractarian novels, sexual love is treated as worthy in itself. The glamour of Inglesant's love for Mary Collet shed a holy radiance on the woods and fields of Little Gidding, and on the convent room where she was dying.[15]

If in form the fiction of Shorthouse represents a point of development somewhat beyond that of any of the other authors we have examined, and yet recalls traits of the earliest Anglo-

[12] Cf. above Chapter X.
[13] E.g. Malvolti finding the Cavaliere sick.
[14] Cf. *John Inglesant,* II, v, 110.
[15] I, xviii.

Catholic tales, the same is also true of some of the ideas presented. Shorthouse is an advocate of very High Anglicanism. He says that in *John Inglesant* he has endeavored to trace the conflict between Culture and Fanaticism, "to depict the Cavalier as not invariably a drunken brute, and spiritual life and growth as not exclusively the possession of Puritans and Ascetics."[16] But he is still hostile to Rome. He allows one of his characters to say that the lamentable condition of Italy arises from the share the priests have in government. "They are cut off from sympathy with their fellows on most points; and their natural inclinations, which cannot be wholly suppressed, are driven into unworthy and mean channels. . . ."[17] In the Introductory Chapter to *John Inglesant,* Geoffrey Monk (of the nineteenth century) goes to a chapel with his Roman Catholic friends and is not convinced "that there was more under that gorgeous ceremonial than may be found under the simpler Anglican ritual of the Blessed Sacrament."[18] Yet the horror of early Tractarian novelists, like William Sewell, for concealed "Papists," has disappeared. The very *hero* is an Anglican who works with the Jesuits, and Mr. Inglesant had nominated as chaplain at the Priory a man who was "ex animo" a Papist, one of the many kept in the English Church by High doctrines and ceremonies—a parallel with this age.[19] It is quite possible that this tolerance must be ascribed to the fashion that fiction should be objective, rather than to the author's convictions, for in a piece of non-fiction Shorthouse has expressed the definite opinion that the Papal system "never was anything but a propagandist machine for extracting forced obedience and alms from

[16] Preface, I, p. x.
[17] II, v, 101.
[18] I, 6.
[19] I, ii, 49.

an ignorant, a deceived, and a terrified world. The Papal Curia . . . As I have said elsewhere, it has always been, and is now, the enemy of the Human Race."[20]

Politically, *John Inglesant* is as pro-Stuart as any Tractarian tale, and seems to preach the Divine Right of Kings. A generation of Anglo-Catholic fiction has accustomed us to such advice as John Inglesant receives from his master: "attach yourself wholly to the King and the Church party, the foundations of whose power are in the Divine will . . . you are not placed here to reason (as the sectaries and the precisians do), but to obey. Remember it is the very seal of a gentleman—to obey. . . ." He speaks of "the voice of God, speaking to you in that rank in which he has placed you, through those captains whom He has ordained to the command. Whenever . . . the Divine Light shall appear to you, be assured it will never teach you anything contrary to this."[21] I suspect reference, perhaps semi-conscious, to the assaults on the Church in Victorian England, in the remark of sixteenth-century Richard Inglesant when some of the lawless poor attack the Priory at the time of its suppression: "A fine piece of work we have set our hands to, with all the rascal people of the country to aid."[22]

In the "Introduction" to the *Life, Letters, and Literary Remains of J. H. Shorthouse,* Smith asks, were not the souls of both Spenser and Shorthouse "ravished with the contemplation of the saint who was also a gentleman?"[23] We have already traced this social type through some of the earlier High Church novels. Shorthouse increases the esthetic and chivalric elements until his ideal becomes almost the saint well-groomed or the

[20] "Preface on the Royal Supremacy" in Arthur Galton's *The Message and Position of the Church of England* (1899), pp. xiii-xiv.
[21] I, ii, 38.
[22] I, i, 22.
[23] I, p. xx.

saint well-born. Molinos going to his trial, "was carefully dressed in his priestly habit,"[24] and at one of the crucial points of his life John Inglesant "was evidently dressed carefully, with a view to the effect to be produced upon a fastidious and ultra-refined assembly. . . . He had, indeed, to one who saw his dress and not his face, entirely the look of a petit-maître, and even—what is more contemptible still—of a petit-maître priest."[25] When Shorthouse suggested publishing this novel in the cheapest edition possible, " 'Oh! no, Henry,' replied his wife; 'remember *John Inglesant* was *always well-dressed.*' And so the book appeared in vellum with gold edges."[26] Women, too, of course, can be saints with taste. The Molinists whom Inglesant is addressing include "ladies in rich attire, yet in whose countenances was seen that refinement of beauty which only religion and holy life can give—ladies, who, while appearing in public in the rank which belonged to them, were capable in private of every self-denial, trained in the practice of devotion and acts of mercy."[27] In *Sir Percival,* the Reverend Charles de Lys "combined in a remarkable degree the characters of a gentleman and of a saint." And the author speaks of "the peculiar combination of the gentleman and the priest which existed in Mr. de Lys."[28] Of Charles Simeon of Cambridge (a real person) Shorthouse says he was a "remarkable instance of the combination of religion with high breeding. His family in the past had been connected with . . ." (and so on).[29]

[24] II, xviii, 356.

[25] II, xvii, 336.

[26] Montgomery, "Some Personal Recollections of Mr. Shorthouse" in *Life, Letters . . . (etc.)* I, 406.

[27] II, xvii, 330.

[28] II.

[29] *Sir Percival,* II.

Snobbery, even snobbery in the older sense of a manner betraying congenital social inferiority, appears in the statement of the narrator of *Blanche, Lady Falaise* that she is in possession of a copy of a letter written by a Duke, "and I have been very much exercised in my mind whether I ought to reveal it to the public or not. It is so genuinely private; it treats upon such very solemn and important subjects relating to the highest classes, that I have long hesitated before finally determining to print it here."[30] The same person outlines a theory of art and society which is implied by Shorthouse's own writings. We see the relation between his admiration for aristocracy and his Platonism. "There is therefore in true art no such thing as realism, for it is just this quality of the hitherto ungrasped which is the ideal, and which alone gives to art any *raison d'être* at all. . . . The things which are seen are temporal, but the things which are unseen are eternal." It is simply assumed that the realm of eternals is aristocratic: "The old world, with its form and guise, is rapidly passing away. A struggle for existence, for daily bread, such as the world has perhaps never seen, is close upon us, and before this struggle palaces and parks, statues and pictures, perchance, will be consumed, as they have been consumed before, in a *lex ignea,* a fiery law, but the eternal will survive. . . . The same types will return again. The Dux, the leader, will reappear. The Norman, the aristocrat, like my Lord Falaise, will come to the front." And on the next page, she speaks of "the old feudal, aristocratic, cultured life that is so rapidly passing away."[31] The logical connection between these ideas may not seem strong. but the connection in prejudice is by this time familiar to us.

[30] I, i, 42.
[31] "Introduction," 1-3.

The Platonism of this Birmingham merchant is that of an esthete. He speaks with approval of a man who:

> escaped, by an instinctive recoil, everything that was coarse, cruel, or unpleasant. His religion consisted in following the good and the beautiful, and he *avoided intuitively the disquieting and difficult aspects both of life and thought.* The existence of beauty was to him a safeguard and an asylum from all the attacks of Satan and of doubt. It led him to a Father in Heaven. To him the long range of white summits were indeed the heavenly Beulah. Every lovely chord, or sunset, or mountain rill, or rocky valley, assured him of a higher life; and safe in this fairyland, he could defy the distracting sights of evil or the insinuating whispers of doubt. [That is why—] His disposition was singularly sweet and placid. . . .[32]

Molinos says to John Inglesant, "How can you, nursed in Courts, delicately reared and bred, trained in pleasure, your ear and eye and sense habituated to music and soft sounds, to colour and to beauty of form, your brain developed by intellectual effort and made sensitive to the slightest touch—how can religious questions bear the same aspect to you as to a man brought up in want of the necessaries of life, hardened by toil and exposure . . .? Yet God is equally with both of these; in His different ways He will lead both of them . . . God is with all, with the coarse and dull as with the refined and pure, but He draws them by different means,—those by terror, these by love."[33] And according to the course of the story, Inglesant is indeed led by love, surrounded with beauty, at home in Courts. Shorthouse, and John Inglesant, are entranced with the beauty of holiness. We have seen little of this before in the Anglo-Catholic novel, except in *The Heir of Redclyffe*,

[32] *The Countess Eve,* VIII, 153-154. (The italics are mine.)
[33] *John Inglesant,* II, v, 110.

but the poetry of John Keble, Coventry Patmore, and Christina Rossetti, shows that it had been part of the Oxford Movement from the beginning.

Kingsley objected to Catholicism on the grounds that it did not make human happiness its aim, and that it preached obedience to the Church rather than to human instinct. Newman, Miss Yonge, Keble, would have considered such an accusation a compliment. Though Shorthouse makes it Puritanism that is opposed to human nature,[34] he defends a Christian rejection of the World: As Inglesant begins to find human life an interesting study, his heart smites him for the luxurious sense of pleasure he finds in the present movement and aspect of things. "Doubtless this human philosophy if we may so call it, into which he was drifting, has a tendency, at least, very different from much of the teaching which is the same in every school of religious thought. Love of mankind is inculcated as a sense of duty by every such school; but by this is certainly not intended love of and acquiescence in mankind as it is.... A world of perfect beings" would lack, for such a man, the vital salt of life, "indignation, sorrow, satire, doubt, restlessness." "But if a man does not desire a perfect world, what part can he have in the Christian warfare?" And, "the pleased acquiescence in life as it is . . . is surely incompatible with following the footsteps of the Divine Ascetic. . . . With all their errors, they who rejected the world and all its allurements, and taught the narrow life of painful self-denial, must be more nearly right than this."[35] This view, indeed all of Inglesant's attempt to lead the good life, shows less interest in a Heaven lying in the future than in a Platonic realm of ideals subsisting eternally, independent of time or space.

[34] I, vi, 121; vii.
[35] II, v, 124-126.

The basis of morality for Shorthouse is not in the human mind. An incident from *Sir Percival* illustrates very clearly that the reason for doing good is not found in conscience, but rather in supernatural commands. Virginia Clare, hearing that an old woman has been attacked by a disease (then epidemic), sets out to visit her, and is accompanied by Constance Lisle. But, on the way, Constance tries to stop her, saying, "I am confident that it is not the will of God that we should go on. The air is full of evil omens. . . ." Virginia says she knows nothing of Constance's spiritual visions, but understands only a commonplace morality which teaches her to visit the helpless and sick. A vague idea forms itself in Constance's mind "that He who originated the visitation of the sick was revealed to some by 'vision of angels.' " Virginia dies of the fever.[36] It will be noticed that this is in accord with the attempt of the whole Oxford Movement to revive supernaturalism, and to combat the "commonplace morality" that determined right and wrong according to merely human conviction. Shorthouse, however, differs from the Tractarians in that he shows the will of God revealing itself through omens and visions, while his predecessors had shown it revealed through a priesthood, and through such prosaic external circumstances as income and rank.

In other words, not only is Anglo-Catholicism in Shorthouse modified, and inextricably intertwined with such allied tendencies as symbolism and estheticism, and with the less closely related current of Platonism; but it is also, at last, mystical. One of the implications of the Oxford Movement is being worked out in fiction almost for the first time, a generation after the Movement began. This is being done in Shorthouse partly with the assistance of other traditions. First, this same Platonism, asserting the reality of a realm beyond that of

[36] VII, VIII.

visible phenomena, is only a step removed from supernaturalism, the belief that such a realm exerts actual force upon the
phenomenal world. The other tradition is that of Quakerism.
Shorthouse comes to Catholicism as a Quaker. It is true that
whereas the Society of Friends has gone farther than any
other body in rejecting the Sacraments, along with the sacer-
dotal system, Shorthouse is a "strong Sacramentalist."[37] *John
Inglesant* gives characteristic emphasis to ritual and to the esthetics of worship.[38] Indeed, Shorthouse seems to go out of his
way to mention ceremonial, especially those features under
attack during the Ritualistic conflict. When Inglesant first sees
the King take the Sacrament, there is a "high altar on which
candles were burning."[39] But Shorthouse is interested in the
Sacraments, particularly in the Sacrament of the Eucharist,
not as a duty or as a sacrificial rite, but primarily as a means of
attaining direct spiritual contact with God. This is, of course,
present in Catholicism, but it is particularly the thing a Quaker
would seize upon. In his reverence for the Inner Light, Shorthouse is not far removed from the Friends.[40] Though he differs
from them in his respect for rank, he is similar in his distrust
of the priesthood, and even of forms themselves as interme-
diaries interposing themselves between the individual and the
direct vision of the Divine.[41] He is still a Quaker in his gentle
quietness, his own utter removal from anything like combat, his
lack of a creed. If the early religious background of Shorthouse seems to have enabled him to achieve a deeper insight

[37] So he defined his own position. Quoted by Montgomery. *Life, Letters
. . . (etc.),* I, 399.
[38] E.g., I, "Introductory Chapter," p. 7; II, xv, 296-7.
[39] I, iv, 80.
[40] E.g., I, ii; I, iv, 88.
[41] Compare the Protestant criticism of Catholicism quoted from Charlotte
Brontë, above, Ch. VIII.

into the true nature of Anglo-Catholicism than its groping adherents had yet attained, it also kept him apart from them in some of their doctrines. The complex system of beliefs that Newman advocates in his novels should be contrasted with the simple, tolerant, undogmatic religion of Shorthouse. A few quotations will illustrate this mysticism and its Quaker-Catholic form.

Inglesant's first schoolmaster tells him to look upon himself as an immortal spirit walking among supernatural things.[42] Mr. Ferrar says that among the Papists, "as among all people, there were many true worshippers of Jesus, being drawn by the blessed Sacrament to follow Him in the spiritual and divine life," and he advises Inglesant to continue seeking the inward spiritual life, "seeking it chiefly in the holy Sacrament accompanied with mortification and confession."[43] After Inglesant has received the bread and wine in the church at Little Gidding, Heaven itself seems to have opened to him.[44] Inglesant later says, "I would willingly believe that God is speaking to me with an immediate voice, nay, more, that I may enter into the very life that God is leading, and partake of his nature."[45]

Indeed, it is the author's eagerness for free access to the supernatural chiefly through the Eucharist, or Mass, which leads him to condemn the Roman Church. He says with reference to the influence of Molinos:

> It appeared for a moment as if Christendom were about to throw off its shackles, its infant swaddling clothes . . . and, acknowledging that the childhood of the Church was past, stand forth before God with her children around her, no longer distrusted

[42] I, iii, 67.
[43] I, iv, 88. (See the whole paragraph.)
[44] I, iv, 96, 97.
[45] I, v, 111.

and enslaved, but each individual complete, fellow-citizens with their mother of the household of God. The unsatisfactory rotation of formal penitence and sinful lapse, of wearisome devotion and stale pleasures, had given place to an enthusiasm which believed that, instead of ceremonies and bowing in outer courts, the soul was introduced into heavenly places, and saw God face to face. A wonderful experience, in exchange for lifeless formality and rule, of communion with the Lord, with nothing before the believer, as he knelt at the altar, save the Lord Himself, day by day, unshackled by penance and confession as heretofore. [On the other hand, "It cannot be denied . . . that freedom of thought as well as of devotion was the motive of numbers who followed the teaching of Molinos."][46]

In the last chapter of the novel, where the author seems to be establishing the view he wishes to leave with the reader, Inglesant, when asked whether he prefers the Romish or Anglican system, says that it is not a dispute between sects and kingdoms but a conflict between the noblest parts of man's nature arrayed against each other: on the one side obedience and faith; on the other, freedom and reason. "I was trained to obedience and devotion; but the reason in my mind for this conduct was that obedience and devotion and gratitude were ideal virtues, not that they benefited the order to which I belonged, nor the world in which I lived. This I take to be the difference between the Papists and myself. The Jesuits do not like Plato [Inglesant's master] as lately they do not like Lord Bacon. Aristotle, as interpreted by the schoolmen, is more to their mind. According to their reading of Aristotle, all his Ethics are subordinated to an end, and in such a system they see a weapon which they can turn to their own purpose of maintaining dogma, no matter at what sacrifice of the individual conscience or reason. This is what the Church of Rome has

[46] II, xvii, 329-330.

ever done. . . . It has based its system upon the profoundest truths, and upon this platform it has raised a power which has . . . played the part of human tyranny. . . . It has, therefore, for the sake of preserving intact its dogma, risked the growth and welfare of humanity, and has, in the eyes of all except those who value this dogma above all things, constituted itself the enemy of the human race." He says that "mankind will do wrong—if it allows to drop out of existence, merely because the position on which it stands seems to be illogical, an agency by which the devotional instincts of human nature are enabled to exist side by side with the rational. The English Church, as established by the law of England, offers the supernatural to all who choose to come . . . the way is open; it is barred by no confession, no human priest."[47]

Though *John Inglesant* shares with the earliest Tractarian fiction many traits, even in unexpected matters of method and thought, it is set apart from them by *fin-de-siècle* characteristics: symbolism, estheticism, mysticism, Neo-Romantic ardour. But these qualities, together with the Platonic and Quaker, rather seemed to aid Shorthouse in giving to Anglo-Catholicism itself worthy artistic expression, not, it is true, unadulterated. For a Modern of entirely secular culture, there would be few more attractive introductions to religion than *John Inglesant*. This novel, for the most part, like *Pilgrim's Progress* and the *Book of Ruth*, speaks immediately to human intuition in terms that are acceptable without regard to the reader's own faith or philosophy.

[47] II, xix, 381-383.

CHAPTER XVI

THE DEVELOPMENT OF METHOD—A SUMMARY

SINCE I have been recording *Geistesgeschichte,* not advocating a philosophy, my tale has been of matter often
rather instructive than glorious. An intuition of deeper realities
than the sense can perceive, the emotion appreciate, or the
intellect understand, is to be conveyed to other minds only
by a higher art than any exploration largely into unremem-
bered literature may hope to discover in abundance. But no
faithful believer ever lets the crimes he reads about in ecclesiastical history weaken his love of spiritual Truths. By the
same token, he will say that the Oxford Movement, as it was
of God, was perfect, but as it was of the world of fact, was
imperfect, and that here we have another illustration that man
is by nature vile and needs the salvation possible only through
a divine Church. Considering the shallowness of most of the
souls with which we have dealt, their narrow scope and cheap
self-satisfaction, it seems to me that we have been rewarded
with more flashes of insight than we had a right to expect. We
have traced the treatment of the Movement in many first-rate
novels of the period, and, to give a background and suggest
general lines of development, in a mass of the most obscure
fiction; observing content, form, tone, and method,—from the
wild revolutionary clash of Chartist times, through the quiet,
almost breathless calm of Mid-Century repose, to the very
dissolution of the age itself. The touches which these novels

have added to the picture of Victorian life and opinion should not be separated from the body of this study, associated as they are with the decades, traditions, and authors that made them. But we may summarize, from the point of view of the novel as novel, the fictional treatment of Anglo-Catholicism, from the beginnings until the masterpiece, *John Inglesant*. The divisions merely mark stages in one continuous evolution.

The fiction we have followed began as controversial tales dealing with such subjects as church restoration, the interpretation of certain Biblical texts, and the adoption of certain old practices. But these tales were especially concerned with saving England from revolution. At first raw one-sided exposition, often provided with footnotes, was fitted into an almost unrelated frame-work of fiction. But by the end of the 'forties there had been a number of experiments in fusing argument with story. Love interest was admitted less grudgingly. Technique, though still ascetic, was less dogmatic, for it was now more common to give both sides of the argument. Within this general development, two figures stood out. Disraeli's narrative method was exactly suited to the New Toryism: a play of radical wit presenting political programs, amidst a setting of aristocratic society. It was a technique that, more sober and somewhat less consciously that of a non-Briton, could have produced a Tractarian masterpiece. Newman allowed his characters to be motivated and his plots determined by the leading of a Kindly Light.

The 'fifties opened with the Papal Aggression, and a change of front and tone. The battle was now less with the Evangelical and more with either the Liberal or the Romanist. This change had begun soon after Newman's secession (1845). But in the 'fifties came the dying down of controversy. For a decade or more the novel was primarily a (not unbiased) photograph of domestic manners. Formerly the subject had been Anglo-Catholic ideas, now it was Anglo-Catholic families. All through this Mid-Victorian half-generation tolerance increased, as the Puseyite grew to hold a recognized place in English life. More and more emphasis was placed on story, character, and humor. The fiction of serious psychological and social study had changed from *deus-ex-machina* causation, to a carefully worked out chain of consequence, and was definitely on the road towards the deterministic technique of the naturalists. Miss Yonge and Miss Sewell by following the method of the 'fifties, won a rank as the leading Tractarian novelists. Kingsley's method followed the general development of the period, but was particularly moulded by his liberal reliance on nature. Trollope, finally, because of his High and Dry preferences, gave us the most insidiously false picture of the Victorian clergymen in so far as it concerns the Oxford Movement. But his novels in spirit and method were perfectly representative of the normal genius of the Mid-Victorian Age.

With the rise of Ritualism in the 'sixties and 'seventies, controversy reappeared, often now not as between authors, but between the participants in the novels. Sometimes the writers seemed almost indifferent to the systems as such, sometimes they violently opposed or defended the Anglo-Catholic as the typical enemy of the Agnostic. Plot gained in importance, and was often even sensational. Stories were built out of motives supplied by Anglo-Catholicism itself. The chief interest became not doctrine nor the minor accidents of courtship, but the inner workings of the heart, under the influence of practices or beliefs such as those of celibacy and confession. The general level of technical skill showed steady progress, with mediocre fiction less and less crude. Psychological analysis, characters with ideas, a growing love of story and description, a more profound, subjective attitude towards fundamental intellectual conflicts, finally led to the Philosophic Romance of Shorthouse. For the novel had grown less and less prosaic, passing from the early legality to the human realism of the middle period, and at last it was drawn into the speculative, esthetic, and mystical currents that were rising to sweep away the older culture.

Victoria had yet twenty years to reign, but the old spirit was fled. Between Mrs. Trollope, when "High Church" meant Protestant, condemning all fervor; and Joseph Henry Shorthouse, when even a sort of Quaker Broad Churchman could be a Sacramentalist and portray the Jesuits as human beings; the Oxford Movement had done its work. *The Vicar of Wrexhill* continued the aristocratic "common sense" of the satirical and social eighteenth century. *John Inglesant* revived the very cadences of the subjective, mystical seventeenth. The contrast between these two novels offers most vivid evidence of one change that had passed over English culture—in the heart of the Century of Science.

APPENDIX

NEALE'S CREATIVE EDITING

PERHAPS the most peculiar work of fiction in English was produced by John Mason Neale (one of the great men of the Oxford Movement). This was nothing less than a de-Protestantized edition of John Bunyan's *Pilgrim's Progress*.[1] In the preface Neale points out that many of Bunyan's incidents were not intended to bear an interpretation in accordance with the teaching of the Church.[2] Consequently he sets out to Catholicize the book.

> The moral right of altering an author's works is denied to an editor. . . . [It is said that] What you now teach, and teach in his name, he would have regarded as falsehood; it is dishonest to use his influence, his talents, his popularity, for the purpose of overthrowing his opinions . . . perhaps, a reasonable defense is found in the following consideration. The author whose works are altered, wished, it is to be assumed, to teach the truth. In the editor's judgment, the alterations have tended to the more complete setting forth that truth:—that is, to the better accomplishment of the author's design. If the editor's views of the truth then are correct, he is justified in what he does: if they are false, he is to be blamed for originally holding them, but cannot be called dishonest for making his author speak what he believes that, with more knowledge, that author would have said.[3]

In short, a man may be blamed for making a mistake, but if his views are indeed orthodox, he is justified in the sort of thing

[1] Published 1853.
[2] P. vii.
[3] Pp. x-xi.

that so enraged the downright Kingsley. It is surprising to see how little Neale found it necessary to alter Bunyan to make him fit for Puseyite homes—a striking proof that great religious genius sticks close to the central part of religious experience. But this type of change is made: Where Bunyan has "heretick," Neale writes "blasphemer."[4] And when Ignorance says that the Gate of the Celestial City will be opened to him because he pays every man his own, prays, fasts, pays tithes, and gives alms, and has left his own country, Neale of course omits the praying, fasting, tithing, and alms-giving.[5] When at Vanity Fair the pilgrims are brought before Judge Hategood, Bunyan says that against Faithful three witnesses came in, "to wit, *Envy, Superstition,* and *Pickthank.*" Neale seems unwilling to speak ill of Superstition and substitutes Self-Indulgence,[6] thus putting a plea for asceticism in the place of Bunyan's profound truth that the religion of Vanity Fair is superstition, and that when the worldly find a non-conformist who prefers to seek the truth, they will call in superstition to put him down.

In making fictioneering scholarship serve his faith, Neale exhibited considerable ingenuity. Besides his "miserable emasculation"[7] of Bunyan, he also wrote *Annals of Virgin Saints By a Priest of the Church of England* (1846), which avowedly makes some slight use of the methods of fiction. The preface says that the lives are derived from the original acts or biographies, "most faithfully translated; with an endeavour, however, to catch their spirit rather than to paraphrase their words. For it is certainly truer,—as giving a truer idea of the

[4] Bunyan 132; Neale, 94.
[5] Bunyan, 162; Neale, 128.
[6] Bunyan, 129; Neale, 92.
[7] So called in Gilfillan, *A Third Gallery of Portraits,* 338, where other possible applications of this fruitful type of editing are suggested.

times,—to describe a real scene by means of an imaginary conversation . . . than, by a spiritless version of the historian's words, to conceal or lower the historian's meaning."[8] Here as in the preface to *Pilgrim's Progress* we have the super-scholarly ideal of achieving "truth" even if it is necessary to alter the record.

[8] Pp. x-xi.

BIBLIOGRAPHY

(Unless otherwise noted, the place of publication is London.)

I. BIBLIOGRAPHIES AND LISTS OF FICTION

Baker, Ernest Albert, *A Guide to the Best Fiction*, N.Y., 1913
   A Guide to Historical Fiction, Lond. and N.Y., 1914
"Bibliographies of Questions of the Day," "The Oxford Movement and the Church Crisis," *The Library Association Record*, I, part 1, May, 1899
Boston Public Library, *Chronological Index to Historical Fiction*, second and enlarged ed., Boston, 1875
Courtney, William Prideaux, *A Register of National Bibliography*, 1905-12
Dixson, Zella Allen, *The Comprehensive Subject Index to Universal Prose Fiction*, N.Y., 1897
Goodrich, Nathaniel L., "Prose Fiction, a Bibliography," *Bulletin of Bibliography*, IV, viii—V, viii, Boston, July, 1906—Jan., 1908
Griswold, W. M., *Descriptive List of Novels*, Cambridge, Mass., 1893
Guille-Allès Library and Museum, *Encyclopaedic Catalogue of the Lending Department*, Guernsey (1889-91)
Lane, William Coolidge, *Catalogue of Works on Ritualism . . . presented by J. H. Treat*, Harvard, 1899
Mercantile Library of Philadelphia, *Bulletin, List of Historical Novels and Didactic and Purpose Novels*, Philadelphia, Oct. 1885—Oct. 1889
Nield, Jonathan, *A Guide to the Best Historical Novels and Tales*, fifth ed., 1929

Northup, Clark Sutherland, *A Register of Bibliographies of the English Language and Literature*, New Haven, 1925

Thomson, Oswald Rhodes Howard, *A Contribution to the Classification of Works of Prose Fiction: Being a Classified and Annotated Dictionary Catalogue of the Works of Prose Fiction in the Wagner Institute Branch of the Free Library of Philadelphia*, Bulletin of the Free Public Library of Philadelphia, second ed., 1904

San Francisco Free Public Library, *Classified English Prose Fiction*, San Francisco, 1891

Walbridge, Earle F., "Romans à Clef with Additions," *N.Y. Public Library Bulletin* (Branch Library Book news) III, ix, Nov., 1926; Supplemented in *The Publisher's Weekly*, N.Y., CXIV, vii, Aug. 18, 1928, and CVII, vi, Feb. 7, 1925

N.B. Titles of novels were also obtained from reviews in religious periodicals: *British Critic, Christian Remembrancer, Church of England Magazine,* and *Dublin Review.*

II. FICTION

In references throughout this book, unless I have inserted "p" for "page" small Roman numerals refer to chapters wherever the large numeral must be used to refer to volume or part.

The first date given is that of the first publication as a book.

A few of these pieces of fiction receive no specific mention in my text, but have formed part of the special background of the discussion.

Agnew, Emily C., *Geraldine: A Tale of Conscience*, 1837-39. References are to ed. Philadelphia, 1839

Alfred Lennox; or, Puseyism unveiled. A Tale for the Times, 1851

Anley, Charlotte, *Earlswood; or, Lights and Shadows of the Anglican Church*, 1852

Armitage, Robert, *Doctor Hookwell; or, The Anglo-Catholic Family*, 1842

Ernest Singleton, 1848

B——, M.E.S., *Experience; or, The Young Church-Woman. a Tale of the Times,* 1854

Borrow, George, *Lavengro: The Scholar—The Gypsy—The Priest,* 1851. References are to Everyman ed., 1906
The Romany Rye, 1857. References are to Everyman ed., 1906

Brontë, Charlotte, *The Professor,* 1857. References are to Everyman ed., 1910
Shirley, 1849. References are to Everyman ed. (1908).
Villette, 1853. References are to Everyman ed. (1909).

Buchanan, Robert Williams, *Foxglove Manor,* 1884
The New Abelard, 1884

Bunyan, John, *The Pilgrim's Progress,* Facsimile reproduction of 1678 ed. Noel Douglas Replicas, 1928

C——, M.A., *Enthusiasm Not Religion,* 1848

The Converts; a Tale of the Nineteenth Century, or Romanism and Protestantism brought to bear in their true light against one another, 1837

Conybeare, William John, *Perversion; or, The Causes and Consequences of Infidelity. A Tale for the Times,* 1856. References are to N.Y. ed., 1856

Disraeli, Benjamin, *Coningsby; or, The New Generation,* 1844
Contarini Fleming. A psychological auto-biography, 1832
Endymion, 1880
Lothair, 1870
Sybil; or, The Two Nations, 1845
Tancred; or, The New Crusade, 1847

Edwards, Mrs. A., *Creeds,* 1859

Elliott, Ruth (pseudonym for Lillie Peck), *Undeceived, Roman or Anglican? a Story of English Ritualism,* 1877

Froude, James Anthony, *The Nemesis of Faith,* 1849
Shadows of the Clouds, 1847

Fullerton, Lady Georgiana Charlotte, *Ellen Middleton,* 1844. References are to ed. Baltimore, 1860
Mrs. Gerald's Niece, 1869

Gresley, William, *Bernard Leslie; or, A Tale of the Last Ten Years*, 1842

Bernard Leslie. Second part, 1859

Church-Clavering; or, The Schoolmaster, 1843 (Vol. XXIV of *The Englishman's Library*)

Clement Walton; or, The English Citizen, 1840 (Vol. I of *The Englishman's Library*). References are to new ed., 1849

Charles Lever; or, The Man of the Nineteenth Century, 1841 (Vol. XV of *The Englishman's Library*)

Guyton, Mrs., see Emma Jane Worboise.

Harris, Elizabeth Furlong Shipton, *From Oxford to Rome; and How it Fared with Some who Lately Made the Journey*, 1847

Rest in the Church, 1848

Heygate, William Edward, *William Blake: or, The English Farmer*, 1848

Howard, Anne, *Mary Spencer: a Tale for the Times*, 1844

Ridley Seldon, or, The Way to Keep Lent. A Tale for the Times, 1845

Howard, Mary Matilda, *Brampton Rectory: or, The Lesson of Life*, 1849

Compton Merivale: Another Leaf from the Lesson of Life, 1850

The Youth and Womanhood of Helen Tyrell, 1854

Ingelow, Jean, *Allerton and Dreux: or, The War of Opinion*, 1851

Jenner, Stephen, *Steepleton; or, High Church and Low Church being the present tendencies of parties in the Church, exhibited in the history of Frank Faithful*, 1847

Kingsley, Charles, *Alton Locke: Tailor and Poet. An Autobiography*, 1850. References are to Macmillan ed., 1902

Hypatia; or, New Foes with an Old Face, 1853

Two Years Ago, Cambridge, 1857. References are to Macmillan ed., 1902

The Water-Babies: a Fairy-Tale for a Land-Baby, 1863

Westward Ho! or The Voyages of Sir Amyas Leigh Knt. . . . in the reign of . . . Queen Elizabeth. Rendered into modern English by C.K. Cambridge, 1855

Yeast. a Problem, 1851. Appeared in different form in *Fraser's Magazine,* vol. XXXVIII, July to Dec., 1848. References are to Macmillan ed., 1902

Kingsley, Henry, *Silcote of Silcotes,* 1867. References are to ed. 1895

   Stretton, 1869

Leith, Mrs. Mary Charlotte Julia, *The Chorister Brothers,* 1867

Linton, Mrs. Eliza Lynn, *Grasp your Nettle,* 1865

   Lizzie Lorton of Greyrigg, 1866

   Realities, 1851

   The True History of Joshua Davidson, 1872

   Under Which Lord? 1879.

Long, Lady Catherine, *Sir Roland Ashton: A Tale of the Times,* 1844. References are to ed. N.Y., 1845

Lynn, Eliza, see Mrs. Linton.

Mant, Walter Bishop, *The Village Choristers,* 1854

Monro, Edward, *Walter the Schoolmaster,* 1854

Neale, John Mason, *Annals of Virgin Saints, By a Priest of the Church of England,* 1846

   (editor) *The Pilgrims Progress of John Bunyan. For the use of Children in the English Church,* Oxford, 1853

   Theodora Phranza: or The Fall of Constantinople, 1857. References are to Everyman ed., 1913, title, *The Fall of Constantinople*

Newman, John Henry, *Callista A Sketch of the Third Century,* 1856. References are to ed. 1873

   Loss and Gain: The Story of a Convert, 1848. References are to sixth ed., 1874

Oliphant, Margaret, *Chronicles of Carlingford The Perpetual Curate,* Edinburgh, 1864. References are to ed. Edinburgh and London, 1865

   Phoebe Junior. A Last Chronicle of Carlingford, 1876

Paget, Francis Edward, *Caleb Kniveton, the Incendiary*, Oxford, 1833

> *The Curate of Cumberworth*, 1859
> *Lucretia; or the Heroine of the Nineteenth Century*, 1868
> *Milford Malvoisin: or, Pews and Pewholders*, 1842
> *The Pageant; or Pleasure and its Price*, 1843
> *St. Antholin's; or Old Churches and New. A Tale for the Times*, 1841
> *The Vicar of Roost*, 1859
> *The Warden of Berkingholt; or, Rich and Poor*, 1843

Paley, Frederick Apthorp, *The Church Restorers: a Tale Treating of Ancient and Modern Architecture and Church Decoration*, 1844

Parsons, Mrs. Gertrude, *Thornberry Abbey, A Tale of the Established Church*, 1846

Peck, Lillie, see Ruth Elliott.

Reade, Charles, *The Cloister and the Hearth. A Tale of the Middle Ages*, 1861. Appeared in different form in *Once a Week*, vol. I, July to Dec., 1859, under title, "A Good Fight." References are to Everyman ed., 1906

> *Griffith Gaunt; or, Jealousy*, 1866. References are to third ed., 1867

Robinson, Frederick William, *Beyond the Church*, 1866

> *High Church*, 1860
> *No Church*, 1861

Rockingham, Sir Charles (pseudonym for Philippe Ferdinand Auguste de Rohan Chabot), *Cécile; or, The Pervert*, 1851

Rockstro, William Smyth, *Abbey Lands*, 1857

Savage, Marmion W., *The Bachelor of the Albany* (1847?). References are to ed. by Bonamy Dobrée in *The Rescue Series*, 1927

Sewell, Elizabeth Missing, *Cleve Hall*, 1855. References are to ed. N.Y., 1855

> *The Experience of Life or Aunt Sarah*, 1852. References are to Tauchnitz ed., Leipzig, 1874

Gertrude, (London?), 1845. References are to fourth American ed., N.Y., 1868

Ivors, 1856

Katherine Ashton, 1854

Margaret Percival, Edited by the Rev. William Sewell, B.D., 1847. References are to ed. Philadelphia, 1847

Ursula A Tale of Country Life, 1858

Sewell, William, *Hawkstone; a Tale of and for England in 184–,* 1845. References are to sixth American ed., N.Y., 1848

Shorthouse, Joseph Henry, *Blanche, Lady Falaise,* 1891. References are to ed. 1892

The Countess Eve, 1888

John Inglesant, Birmingham, 1880. References are to ed. London, 1881

Sir Percival: A Story of the Past and the Present, 1886

Skene, Felicia Mary Francis, *S. Alban's; or, the Prisoners of Hope,* 1853

Smith, Eliza, *Clarendon: A Tale of Recent Times,* 1848

Tayler, Charles Benjamin, *Margaret, or the Pearl,* 1844. References are to ed. N.Y., 1846

Thackeray, William Makepeace, *The Newcomes Memoirs of a Most Respectable Family,* in parts, 1853-1855. References are to Charterhouse ed., vols. V. VI, 1901

The History of Pendennis, in parts, 1848-1850. References are to Everyman ed., 1910

Trevor: or, the New St. Francis a Tale for the Times, 1847

Trollope, Anthony, *Barchester Towers,* 1857. References are to Everyman ed., 1906

The Claverings, 1867. References are to ed. in *The World's Classic Series,* 1924

Doctor Thorne, 1858. References are to Everyman ed., 1908

Framley Parsonage, 1861. References are to Everyman ed., 1906

The Last Chronicle of Barset, 1867. References are to Everyman ed., 1909

Rachel Ray, 1863

The Small House at Allington, 1864. References are to Everyman ed., 1909

The Warden, 1855. References are to Royal ed., Philadelphia, 1900

Trollope, Mrs. Frances Milton, *The Vicar of Wrexhill,* 1837

Whately, Elizabeth Jane, *Cousin Mabel's Experiences of Ritualism,* (1867)

Wilford, Florence, *Vivia, A Modern Story,* 1870

Wilkinson, William Francis, *The Parish Rescued: or laymen's duties, rights, and dangers,* 1845

The Rector in Search of a Curate, 1843

Worboise, Emma Jane (Mrs. Guyton), *Amy Wilton, or lights and shades of Christian life,* Bath (1852)

Overdale; or, The Story of a Pervert (But subtitle used at top of alternative pages is *A Tale for the Times*), 1869

Yonge, Charlotte Mary, *Abbeychurch or Self-Control and Self-Conceit,* 1844. References are to second ed., 1872

The Clever Woman of the Family, 1865. References are to Tauchnitz ed., Leipzig, 1865

The Daisy Chain; or Aspirations, 1856

Dynevor Terrace; or The Clue of Life, 1857. References are to ed. N.Y., 1857

The Heir of Redclyffe, 1853. References are to Everyman ed. (1909)

Hopes and Fears; or, Scenes from the Life of a Spinster, 1860

The Pillars of the House; or, Under Wode under Rode, 1873

The Three Brides, 1876

The Trial: More Links of the Daisy Chain, 1864

The Young Curate, or The Quicksands of Life, 1859

III. NON-FICTION, ORIGINAL SOURCES

Disraeli, Benjamin, *Church and Queen,* 1865 (Five speeches delivered 1860-64)

"General Preface" in *Collected Edition of the Novels and Tales,* I, 1870

Hansard, Thomas Carson (editor), *Parliamentary Debates.* Third series, CLXXI (1863) and CCXXI (1874)

Keble, John, *The Christian Year: Thoughts in Verse for the Sundays and Holydays Throughout The Year,* Oxford, 1827

National Apostasy Considered in A Sermon Preached in St. Mary's, Oxford Before His Majesty's Judge of Assize, On Sunday July 14, 1833. Oxford, 1833

Lives of the English Saints written by various hands at the suggestion of John Henry Newman afterwards Cardinal. N.Y., 1903

Lyra Apostolica, Derby, 1836

Newman, John Henry, *Apologia Pro Vita Sua,* The Two Versions of 1864 and 1865 Preceded by Newman's and Kingsley's Pamphlets. With an Introduction by Wilfred Ward, 1913. (Unless otherwise indicated, references are to 1865 version.)

Certain Difficulties Felt by Anglicans in Catholic Teaching Considered: In a Letter Addressed to the Rev. E. B. Pusey, D.D., on occasion of his Eirenicon of 1864 (etc.) 1876

Correspondence of John Henry Newman with John Keble and Others, 1839-1845, 1917

Difficulties Felt by Anglicans in Catholic Teaching Considered. Fourth ed. (1872)

An Essay in Aid of a Grammar of Assent, 1870

Letters and Correspondence of John Henry Newman During his Life in the English Church. Ed. by Anne Mozley (including autobiographical memoir down to 1832), 1891

Perceval, A. P., *A Collection of Papers Connected with the Theological Movement of 1833,* 1842

Sewell, Elizabeth Missing, *The Autobiography of Elizabeth M. Sewell*, Ed. by Eleanor L. Sewell, 1907

Shorthouse, Joseph Henry, "Preface on the Royal Supremacy," in Arthur Galton's *The Message and Position of the Church of England*, 1899

Tracts for the Times, 1834-41

Trollope, Anthony, *An Autobiography*, Lond., 1883. References are to ed., N.Y., 1883

N.B. See also material in books listed under Biographical Studies, below, section V.

IV. SECONDARY AUTHORITIES, GENERAL

Cazamian, Louis, *Le Roman Social en Angleterre*, Paris, 1904

Cazamian, Madeleine, *Le Roman et les Idées en Angleterre. L'Influence de la Science (1860-90)*, Strasbourg, 1923

Church, R. W., *The Oxford Movement Twelve Years 1833-1845*, 1891

Cornish, Francis Warre, *The English Church in the Nineteenth Century*, 1910

Cross, Wilber Lucius, *The Development of the English Novel*, N.Y., set up 1899; references are to seventh impression, 1905

The Eighteen-Seventies (Essays by Fellows of the Royal Society of Literature), ed. by Harley Granville-Barker, N.Y., 1929

Eliot, George, "Silly Novels by Lady Novelists," *The Westminster Review*, New Series, X, xx, Oct., 1856

Escott, Thomas Hay Sweet, *Social Transformations of the Victorian Age. A Survey of Court and Country*, 1897

Foster, Alfred Edye Manning, *Anglo-Catholicism* (1914)

Graves, Charles L., *Mr. Punch's History of Modern England*, 1921-22

Hunt, John, *Religious Thought in England in the Nineteenth Century*, 1896

Hutton, W. H., "The Oxford Movement," *The Cambridge History of English Literature*, XII, Cambridge, 1915, Ch. xii

Inge, William Ralph, *The Platonic Tradition in English Religious Thought* (The Huslean lectures at Cambridge, 1925-26), 1926

Jeaffreson, John Cordy, *Novels and Novelists, From Elizabeth to Victoria,* 1858

Knox, Wilfred, *The Catholic Movement in the Church of England,* 1923

"The Moral Character of Story Books," *The Christian Remembrancer,* XL, cix, July, 1860

Phillips, Walter C., see under Reade, section V

"Religious Stories," *Fraser's Magazine,* XXXVIII, ccxxiv, Aug., 1848

Russell, Mrs. Frances Theresa Peet, *Satire in the Victorian Novel,* N.Y., 1920

Selby, Thomas G., *The Theology of Modern Fiction,* 1897

Selwyn, Edward Gordon (editor), *Essays Catholic and Critical By Members of the Anglican Communion,* N.Y., 1926

Shuster, George N., *The Catholic Spirit in Modern English Literature,* N.Y., 1922, reprint 1925

Speare, Morris Edmund, *The Political Novel Its Development,* N.Y., 1924

Stewart, Herbert Leslie, *A Century of Anglo-Catholicism,* N.Y., (1929)

Stoddard, Francis Hovey, *The Evolution of the English Novel,* N.Y., 1900

Storr, Vernon F., *The Development of English Theology in the Nineteenth Century, 1800-1860,* 1913

Thureau-Dangin, Paul, *La Renaissance Catholique en Angleterre au XIXᵉ Siècle,* Paris, 1899-1906. Translated unreliably as: *The English Catholic Revival in the Nineteenth Century.* "Revised and Re-edited from a Translation by the late William Wilberforce," 1914. This is more flattering to smug susceptibilities than the French original, and is perhaps better adapted to advance the Catholic cause in England. E.g., the original says that in the slums of London there "grouillait une population misérable et sauvage avec laquelle la plupart des ministres anglicans de l'ancien type s'étaient sentis trop *gentlemen* pour se commettre et qui, par suite, vivait en dehors de toute influence chrétienne" (III, 343). The translation says, "there swarmed a miserable and savage population, with which the Anglican ministers of the old type did not mix, and which, in consequence, lived outside all Christian influence." (II, 451)

Trevelyan, George Macaulay, *British History in the Nineteenth Century,* eighth impression, 1928

Tulloch, John, *Movements of Religious Thought in Britain During the Nineteenth Century.* (Fifth series of St. Giles Lectures), 1885

Yonge, C. Fortescue, "English Clergy in Fiction," *The Gentleman's Magazine,* CCLXXXIII, mcmxcix, July, 1897

Wakeling, G., *The Oxford Church Movement; sketches and recollections,* 1895

Walker, Hugh, *The Literature of the Victorian Era,* Cambridge, 1910

Wilson, S. L., *The Theology of Modern Literature,* Edinburgh, 1899

Wingfield-Stratford, Esmé, *The Victorian Tragedy,* 1930

N.B. Of course I have also employed such standard works as Halkett and Laing's *Anonymous and Pseudonymous English Literature, Hastings' Encyclopedia of Religion and Ethics,* Elton, Allibone, D.N.B., etc.

V. BIOGRAPHICAL STUDIES

Church

Life and Letters of Dean Church, edited by Mary C. Church, 1894

Disraeli

Monypenny, William Flavelle, and George Earle Buckle, *The Life of Benjamin Disraeli, Earl of Beaconsfield,* N.Y., 1910-20

More, Paul Elmer, "Disraeli and Conservatism," in *Aristocracy and Justice* (*Shelburne Essays Ninth Series*), 1915

Eliot

George Eliot's Life as related in her Letters and Journals arranged and edited by her husband, J. W. Cross, N.Y., 1885

Keble

Lock, Walter, *John Keble*, 1893

Kingsley

Charles Kingsley, His Letters, and Memories of his Life, edited by his wife, second ed., 1877

Manning

Hemmer, L'Abbé Hippolyte M., *Vie du Cardinal Manning*, Paris, 1898

Morris

Mackail, J. W., *The Life of William Morris*, 1922 (new impression of ed. 1912)

Neale

Gilfillan, George, "Neale and Bunyan" in *A Third Gallery of Portraits*, Edinburgh, 1854

Towle, Eleanor A., *John Mason Neale, D.D.* 1906

Newman

Gates, Lewis E., "Newman as a Prose Writer," in *Three Studies in Literature*, N.Y., 1899

Goyau, Mme. Lucie Félix (Faure), *Newman; sa vie & ses oeuvres*, Paris, 1901

Hutton, Richard Holt, *Cardinal Newman*, 1905

Lilly, W. S., "Anglicanism old and new," *The Dublin Review*, CXXXVIII, cclxxvi, Jan., 1906

Meynell, Wilfred, *Cardinal Newman*, 1907

More, Paul Elmer, "Cardinal Newman," in *The Drift of Romanticism* (*Shelburne Essays Eighth Series*), Boston, 1913

Newman, Francis William, *Contributions Chiefly to the Early History of the Late Cardinal Newman*, 1891

Reilley, Joseph J., *Newman as a Man of Letters*, N.Y., 1925
Sarolea, Charles, *Cardinal Newman and His Influence on Religious Life and Thought*, Edinburgh, 1908
Ward, Wilfred Philip, *The Life of John Henry Cardinal Newman*, 1912

Pusey

Liddon, Henry Parry, *The Life of Edward Bouverie Pusey*, 1893-98

Reade

Coleman, John, *Charles Reade As I Knew Him*, 1903
Phillips, Walter C., *Dickens, Reade and Collins, Sensation Novelists*, N.Y., 1919
Reade, Charles L., and Compton Reade, *Charles Reade Dramatist, Novelist, Journalist   A Memoir Compiled Chiefly from His Literary Remains*, 1887

Shorthouse

Fleming, W. K., "Some Truths about 'John Inglesant,' " *The Quarterly Review*, CCXLV, cdlxxxv, July, 1925
Life, Letters, and Literary Remains of J. H. Shorthouse, ed. by his wife, 1905 (Has an Introduction by J. H. Smith)
More, Paul Elmer, "J. H. Shorthouse" in *Shelburne Essays, Third Series*, 1905

Trollope

Escott, Thomas Hay Sweet, *Anthony Trollope, his Public Services, Private Friends, and Literary Originals*, 1913
Sadleir, Michael, *Trollope. A Commentary*, 1929
Walpole, Hugh, *Anthony Trollope*, 1928

Yonge

Coleridge, Christabel, *Charlotte Mary Yonge Her Life and Letters*, 1903
Romanes, Ethel, *Charlotte Mary Yonge An Appreciation*, 1908